The Fabian Society

The Fabian Society is Britain's leading left of centre think tank and political society, committed to creating the political ideas and policy debates which can shape the future of progressive politics.

With over 300 Fabian MPs, MEPs, Peers, MSPs and AMs, the Society plays an unparalleled role in linking the ability to influence policy debates at the highest level with vigorous grassroots debate among our growing membership of over 7000 people, 70 local branches meeting regularly throughout Britain and a vibrant Young Fabian section organising its own activities. Fabian publications, events and ideas therefore reach and influence a wider audience than those of any comparable think tank. The Society is unique among think tanks in being a thriving, democratically-constituted membership organisation, affiliated to the Labour Party but organisationally and editorially independent.

For over 120 years Fabians have been central to every important renewal and revision of left of centre thinking. The Fabian commitment to open and participatory debate is as important today as ever before as we explore the ideas, politics and policies which will define the next generation of progressive politics in Britain, Europe and around the world. Find out more at **www.fabian-society.org.uk**

Fabian Society
11 Dartmouth Street
London SW1H 9BN
www.fabian-society.org.uk

 Fabian ideas
Series editor: Jonathan Heawood

First published June 2005

ISBN 0 7163 0616 6
ISSN 1746-1146

British Library Cataloguing in Publication data.
A catalogue record for this book is available from the British Library.

Printed by Bell & Bain, Glasgow

Why Life Chances Matter

FABIAN SOCIETY

Acknowledgements

This collection brings together the interim report of the Fabian Commission on Life Chances and Child Poverty and the texts of the Fabian Life Chances lecture series, held in March 2005, along with a new introduction by Sunder Katwala, and responses to the lectures by Polly Toynbee, Lisa Harker, Victor Adebowale, Geoff Whitty and Sukhvinder Stubbs. The Fabian Society would like to thank all the contributors for putting such enthusiasm into this project, and the sponsors of the Life Chances lecture series for their support: Pre-School Learning Alliance; Turning Point; British Property Federation; VT Education; Groundwork; and the Institute of Education for hosting the lectures.

The Fabian Commission on Life Chances and Child Poverty is kindly supported by the Barrow Cadbury Trust, the Sutton Trust, the Webb Memorial Trust and the Dartmouth Street Trust. Without their commitment to supporting independent and original research its work would not be possible. The Commissioners would like to thank the Fabian Secretariat to the Commission: Louise Bamfield, Sadia Haider and Richard Brooks; as well as Sunder Katwala, Jonathan Heawood and the other staff at the Fabian Society. The Commissioners would like to thank the qualitative research staff at MORI, particularly Julian Thompson and Sarah Castell, for their invaluable expertise and timely assistance with the deliberative research aspect of this project. Our thanks also go to the many other people and organisations which have given input.

The views expressed in the interim report are the responsibility of the Commissioners alone and do not necessarily represent the views of the sponsors or any other organisation or individual that has assisted the Commission in its work.

Contents

The Commission comprises the following members:

The Fabian Life Chances Lectures were delivered by the following:

Part One

The Third Term Challenge

The Third Term Challenge
Sunder Katwala

The mission to improve and equalise life chances defines the political left. That is the central argument of this collection. The Labour government's stated ambition is to embed a 'progressive consensus' in British politics and society. If it is to succeed, it will need to give a sharper public account of 'Labour Britain' — how the country it is seeking to create differs from the unequal Britain which Labour inherited and governs today. That is why the Fabian Society, on the eve of the 2005 campaign, invited leading ministers to set out a positive life chances agenda, and to debate their vision in post-lecture debates with leading opinion formers.

The Life Chances lecture series, and the work of the Fabian Life Chances Commision, articulate a clear progressive purpose for Labour's third term. The speeches are at times strikingly frank in acknowledging just how much Labour has still to do. They set out the progress made on employment and the minimum wage and the attack on child and pensioner poverty. But a clear critique of the limits, as well as the scope, of New Labour's first eight years is implicit in David Miliband's analysis that having 'proven competence' and 'delivered progress' in its first and second terms, it will take the third term to 'decide whether this is a realigning government'. Miliband's central argument, in opening the lecture series, that 'inequality in life chances defines the moral, economic and social agenda we face' was developed across the range of policy areas in subsequent lectures. For John Reid, a politics of empowerment is central to narrowing health inequalities; Ruth Kelly argues that the evidence of stalled social mobility demonstrates the need for education reform, citing Anthony Crosland's vision of comprehensive education as an engine of social equality; Alan Milburn argues that a third Labour victory, marking a historic defeat for Thatcherism, must enable progressives to break the glass ceiling on opportunity; and Yvette Cooper offers a powerful analysis of why Labour must do more to mobilise public support for an attack on inequality, as well as poverty and social exclusion.

Governments face many demands and pressures. Of course, administrative competence is necessary; being trusted to run a strong economy is vital, and being able to win support and sustain a progressive government over time is essential. Yet the argument here is that all of these, however challenging in themselves, ultimately remain merely means to an end. For progressives, the fundamental test of a Labour government is how far it can be judged to have reduced inequality in life chances, by improving and spreading opportunities.

This is, rightly, to set the bar high. The jury is out on how far the third term will now deliver on this ambition. This introduction seeks to assess the implications for the politics of life chances of the 2005 General Election. The election presented what could be seen as three reasons for sober pessimism about the prospects for a life chances-centred third Labour term: firstly, the life chances narrative and analysis was too often missing from the election campaign; secondly, a narrower majority and the electoral landscape of 2009 will make a substantive life chances agenda more difficult to pursue; and thirdly, the government's post-election response has not, to date, put tackling inequality at the heart of its third term political and policy narrative. Each of these are central questions to be contested in the post-election debate about the future direction of both the Labour government and the Labour party

In the long campaign of 2005, voters heard much of the dangers of immigration, and the threat of the MRSA bug, and were able to read every dot and comma of the Attorney General's legal advice, as the debate over Iraq, trust and leadership took centre stage. There was a campaign day devoted to ending global poverty but Labour's most transformative domestic ambition - to abolish child poverty at home within a generation - was never central to the campaign script. The pre-election deliberative research carried out by MORI and the Fabian Society (reported in Chapter Two below) found no participant aware of the pledge to eradicate child poverty. It is hard to believe that the election campaign will have done anything to change that.

So how could issues of life chances and equality be more central to the hurly-burly of a future election campaign? There were important progressive themes in this election: we need to learn from and emulate these successes. Most strikingly, the banishment of Howard Flight from Conservative politics ratified Labour's success in making public services trump tax cuts. It was now the right which unwillingly accepted the spending plans of the centre-left—a mirror image of Labour's 1997 decision that it must live with Conservative levels of underinvestment for two years after winning power. Labour was strong when campaigning on its economic record and public services but lacks an equally resonant narrative to address inequality and opportunity. The scope of the life chances agenda will depend on how far the party can develop this in the years ahead of the 2009 election.

The second challenge is that Labour's narrower majority and the electoral landscape of 2009 could make a substantive life chances agenda more difficult to pursue. The 2005 result may well strengthen those who argue this case. A slimmer majority—along with Labour's success in holding a number of the less likely 1997 gains—presents a rather traditional two-party electoral frontline fought in the south and south-east and in relatively affluent seats elsewhere in Britain. The electoral focus will be ever more strongly on voters in Gillingham, Hove, Dartford, Finchley, Harlow, South Dorset, Chester, Selby and other 'supermarginals'.

Yet the Labour party did lose votes, and seats, in 2005 by failing to articulate its progressive social justice agenda effectively enough. In particular, the party's response to the electoral challenge of the Liberal Democrats, who made an effective appeal for Labour protest votes, was too weak. While Labour lost 31 seats to the Conservatives, the LibDems can claim a clear 'assist' and much of the credit for 15 of these seats, where the rise in LibDem share was larger than the Conservative majority, and there was a similar phenomenon in several of the 'supermarginals' narrowly held by Labour which would be lost to the Conservatives on a 2.5 per cent swing next time. Far too much of Labour's response to the LibDems came from a tired playbook template of attack lines from the right. Attacking the LibDems as weak on crime, soft on drugs and high on tax, as the party had done in a number of late-90s by-elections, proved particularly ill-suited to the politics of 2005. By focusing very heavily on a psephological argument ('Don't let Michael Howard in'), Labour too often seemed to accept the perception of the LibDem policy programme as more progressive, rather than mounting what could have been a highly effective challenge on social justice grounds by comparing the redistribu-tive impact of Labour's policies overall with a critique of the LibDem proclivity for middle-class welfarism.

It is not to propose any 'lurch to the left' to recognize that a good proportion of disillusioned progressive voters had relatively high levels of political engagement and required a considerably more sophisticated political message than was offered to them. Labour's electoral success will depend in part on winning back the progressive voters who formed part of its electoral coalition in 1997 and 2001. Because the next election will be won in the centre, Labour's ability to pursue its life chances agenda will depend on how far it can, before 2009, shift the political centre ground.

But the government's immediate post-election response has so far not suggested that the agenda of tackling inequality will be more central in Labour's third term narrative. The focus on the politics of respect and civility, for example, address public concerns about crime and social disorder which have an important impact on quality of life, especially for the worst-off. Having started a post-election national debate about

5

that topic, the government may be seen to imply that Labour's fundamental critique of contemporary British society is that there has been a mystifying decline in respect about which something must be done. If the links are not made to a broader agenda of supporting communities, tackling inequality and identifying the role of public provision, then this risks being a rather thin, conservative agenda, and the government will fail to mobilise support for an effective progressive response both to crime and anti-social behaviour and to social policy as a whole.

There has long been a debate within the party about the need for Labour to make more of its social justice achievements since 1997. The counter-argument has been that 'social democracy by stealth' is better than no social democracy at all. Labour has delivered results through a strategy of (sometimes surprisingly radical) 'progressive change without frightening the horses' and retained office while its continental European sister parties have lost. This strategy is increasingly contested in the debate about how the party now evolves and renews itself in office. If we do not accept that we have already reached the boundaries of the possible in delivering progressive change — that Labour can make progress in power but can not in fact realign the centre of British political gravity — then the central challenge is to define a credible public narrative, policy agenda and political strategy which can see the government successfully 'go public' with its social justice agenda. How can this be done?

Firstly, Labour ministers must start a new 'Condition of Britain' debate designed to put inequality and life chances at the centre of the public political agenda. Governments have a good deal of power to choose which national debates to start — what Americans call the use of the 'bully pulpit'. In this case, Labour ministers must create awareness of the problem which they are seeking to tackle if they wish to mobilise support and resources necessary to achieve their policy goals.

This will require an increased willingness to talk about class in Britain today. The goal of equal life chances was described by Alan Milburn in our lecture series as 'an open, mobile classless society'. But achieving this goal of classlessness depends on a more explicit recognition of just how important class remains in structuring British society. As the Fabian Commission research shows, there is widespread ignorance, even denial, of this. If it is the life chances and inequality agenda which motivates Labour politicians in power, then they will need to present the evidence to the British public that inequality is a defining yet corrosive feature of British society. That would open up the argument that tackling intergenerational transmission of poverty and disadvantage is an essential part of what a fair society would demand. Such an agenda would also see mutual respect as an important component of a shared society – it would make reasonable demands of the responsibilities of citizenship at both the top and the bottom of the pile.

Secondly, at the level of policy, renewing the government in power depends on being clearer about the political and ideological approach which underpins the policy decisions which the government makes, and on how these fit together. A 'life chances' litmus test for policy could be particularly useful in both policy formulation and in the public political definition of what the government is doing and why. Under the Thatcher government, civil servants were clear that the ideological focus of the government would be to ask whether a particular proposal would deliver a smaller state. For Labour, the equivalent question should be 'how will this help improve and equalise life chances?'.

This would clarify, for example, that the debate about choice in public services is properly about means rather than ends. Progressives should support choice mechanisms which improve the outcomes and life chances of the disadvantaged - who are worst-served by the services we have – while questioning those which have a negative impact on life chances and equality. It is therefore an approach which could help the party to navigate difficult and controversial debates – such as those over university funding or NHS reform. It would also help the party debate its priorities in what is likely to be a tighter public spending environment, through a 'life chances' perspective on the priorities for the next spending review.

Thirdly, the challenge of political mobilisation is to unite Labour's electoral coalition around a government with greater confidence in its ability to articulate the progressive purposes which motivate it. The politics of the 2005 election were, in part, the consequence of a historic imbalance of confidence in British politics—a legacy of the long Conservative century which Labour has successfully broken. Yet a largely unreconstructed political right did so much to set the agenda over the first five months of 2005, even as it cruised to a universally predicted third successive defeat. It is because the Conservative Party has retained rather too much confidence for its own good that it has taken eight years to begin any proper inquest into its recurrent defeats, or to develop any substantive analysis of New Labour's political successes, beyond believing it to be a mirage which will one day disappear as the political pendulum swings back to the natural party of government.

Yet this seems too often mirrored on the Labour side. Were the scars of the party's long years in the wilderness and traumatic 1992 defeat so deep as to make New Labour's DNA incapable of confidence, still less complacency? To date, New Labour has defined itself negatively as much as positively. The politics of grievance will inevitably affect any incumbent government. A government in power for a decade can no longer rely on defining itself against either a caricature of the political left or solely on fading memories of its opponents' failures when last in office. Embedding a progressive consensus depends on being able to define the government's political and policy agenda positively and clearly. This will require greater confidence in the government's ability to make the political weather—and indeed to set the terms of debate for the post-election inquests of the other parties if the party is to embed change for a generation or more.

The life chances agenda offers Labour the opportunity to articulate its vision of the good society, and the programme which can bring that society closer to reality. It is on this that the government's sustained political success depends.

Part Two

Life Chances:
What the public really think
about poverty

The Fabian Commission
Interim Report

1 | Introduction

The abolition of child poverty in the UK would transform our society. To achieve this by 2020 is by far the most ambitious — yet one of the least recognised — of all the commitments which the Labour government has made. It is a commitment unmatched by the other major political parties.

Five years on, a quarter of the task has been achieved. But while taking a million children out of poverty is a major achievement in itself, there remains a long way to go. There were four million children living in poverty in Britain in 1998. There are still some three million today.

The task will only get harder from now on. In part this is because of the sheer scale of current poverty and inequality in the UK. It is also because of the vicious cycle whereby poverty in childhood is the fore-runner of poor health, education and other key outcomes in adulthood. If we are to break the cycle of disadvantage by which children who grew up in poverty continue to experience poverty as parents we will have to tackle the deep and prevalent inequalities in our society. Some people will be hard to reach because they suffer from multiple and severe disadvantage.

However, there is another group which will prove 'hard to reach' too — the broader public. By European standards the UK public is uniquely misinformed about the extent of poverty in the UK. We are also much more likely to believe that poverty is caused by behavioural factors—something captured in the strength of negative stereotypes of the poor. A great many people still need to be convinced both that there is real poverty in Britain today, and that it is possible to do something about it. Our research shows that it is hard for many people to believe that poverty exists in the midst of our affluent society. They think there must be something wrong with the parents of children who suffer from material deprivation. They do not know about the government's commitment to end child poverty. They are startled to discover that other European countries have successfully chosen not to tolerate it.

The Fabian Commission on Life Chances and Child Poverty seeks to influence and inform the government's strategy. We do not believe that poverty can be abolished by stealth. We believe this can only be achieved by reshaping the wider political and public debates about poverty and inequality in Britain. At the moment there is insufficient public consent for the necessary scale of change. This consent must become part of a new settlement, a new political consensus, if the decision not to accept poverty in our society is to prove as politically robust as Clement Attlee's National Health Service became after 1951.

Before we can persuade people about the importance of tackling poverty and inequality, we need to be clear about what we are trying to achieve and why. This means sorting out the confused debate around equality, social mobility, and meritocracy. The Commission believes that the concept of life chances helps to clarify this muddle. Our vision is of a society without child poverty, and where all children have more equal chances of achieving decent outcomes as they progress through life.

What does the left, and the Labour Party, think today about equality? Tony Blair was famously unwilling to answer Jeremy Paxman's question in the 2001 election campaign about whether it was acceptable for the gap between the rich and the poor to get wider. But at the same time the government has tried—with some success—to close the gap in school achievement between children in different social classes, and recognises the need to tackle health inequalities. Politicians now need to be confident about publicly making the links between different policies designed to tackle disadvantage. We think that life chances provides the right framework through which to do so.

It is often said that New Labour is in favour of equality of opportunity, but what this means is rarely spelled out. Bare formal equality of opportunity — 'a fair race' — still allows some to start with powerful and often inherited advantages. The Commission argues that life chances is a more useful and more compelling concept than equality of opportunity. It combines a concern about opportunities with a concern about the factors that affect opportunities. It also embodies the idea of a flourishing society in which every child enjoys an equal start in life and opportunities at every stage of their development.

Social mobility is a key issue for politicians at the moment, partly because of recent evidence that it is becoming more difficult for children to progress from disadvantaged backgrounds. In theory, concern about social mobility reflects a very important idea: that we should be concerned not only with poverty — the floor below which no-one should fall — but also with the distribution of opportunities across society. In practice, however, the meaning of the term is not always clear. Too often it is used as shorthand for a vague notion of 'getting on in the world' and at its worst social mobility can simply mean creating narrow ladders out of disadvantage for the lucky few. We believe that if it is narrowly about increasing the opportunities for gifted and aspiring individuals from 'poor' backgrounds then it fails to capture most of what is morally important about a fair distribution of chances in life.

So how do we start to make a public argument? Our deliberative research demonstrated the scale of the challenges. But we also witnessed some encouraging shifts of opinion and gained some important evidence on which an effective public strategy must build. Stark evidence of material deprivation — of one in 50 children in 1999 going without a warm coat, and one in 25 missing out on a birthday celebration — proved to be the 'killer facts' in overturning a strong initial prejudice that 'poverty' was being applied to those who lacked only this year's mobile phone or trainers. However, once engaged in this way our participants quickly recognised other arguments about the effects of poverty on children's later chances in life, and about the inefficiency of wasting their future potential.

Our workshop participants were—without exception—unaware that the government was seeking to end child poverty in the UK. However, once activated by the evidence, they were engaged and enthused by the pledge—particularly because of the impressive evidence of the record to date. It seemed to us that this was the government's 'best kept secret', and something which could prove highly effective in re-engaging Labour's core vote, though our research found the pledge to take all children out of poverty in fact appealed right across the political spectrum. Indeed, it was Labour's record to date which proved a key factor in our participants all saying that they would personally contribute more—in higher taxes—to help eradicate poverty.

We also asked our workshop participants about their attitudes towards focusing public services on the disadvantaged. Their view here was they would not accept any worsening of their own services as the price of improving services for others. What they would accept was slower improvement in their own services if this enabled faster progress for the disadvantaged. In other words, our participants were prepared to see public services used to level up inequalities.

The messages for politicians are clear. It is unacceptable that the children of people living in poverty have systematically worse chances in life than the children of the rich. Those who wish to abolish child poverty need to go public about their ambitions. They should use the evidence of success so far to build public confidence that the issue really can be addressed. They should combat the stereotypes of 'the poor' that sap public support. They should be more confident in talking about inequality, and clearer about the language they use. Life chances is the right framework. As a first step, Labour should make a manifesto pledge at the next General Election to take one million more children out of poverty by 2010. When Jeremy Paxman asks the question about inequality once again, the answer should be: 'Yes, the gap does matter. By improving the chances of the disadvantaged I want to narrow the gap between the rich and the poor.'

This report is structured around the results of original deliberative research carried out by MORI for the Commission in February 2005. The first section sets out what we now know as a result of this work about public attitudes towards poverty in the UK today, what the reality of poverty is, and how the MORI participants reacted to exposure to this information. The second section discusses life chances and the politics of equality, and how the MORI participants reacted to exposure to arguments and information about life chances. The final section draws conclusions about how politicians and other public figures should go about making the public case for tackling poverty and inequality.

2 | Attitudes towards poverty and life chances

We do not yet have a particularly strong or nuanced understanding of public attitudes towards poverty and inequality, of what people believe to be the perceived causes of poverty and inequality, and what the public think about the policies that seek to address them. The worry amongst politicians is that in the privacy of the ballot box principled concern for the gap between rich and poor often gives way to a more individualistic set of concerns about one's own household finances. Indeed, the survey evidence provides some confirmation of the conventional wisdom that a sizeable gap exists between general professions of support for higher spending on the most disadvantaged and readiness to part with the cash in reality.[i] To gain a better understanding of these issues, the Fabian Commission engaged MORI to undertake a qualitative research project on public attitudes towards child poverty and life chances.[ii] The sample was chosen to be broadly representative in terms of age, gender and ethnicity, but generally excluded people on either end of the left/right political spectrum. We wanted to find out what people in the political centre ground thought about poverty and inequality.

Some of the findings we report here may seem depressing—and difficult territory from which to start to put together a compelling public and political case. There was much initial scepticism about the mere existence of poverty in the UK, a very strong belief that 'bad parenting' is the most important cause of what child poverty there is, and virtually no knowledge whatsoever of the government's ambition to address the issue. Yet we also witnessed some highly encouraging shifts of opinion—anger at evidence of real deprivation in Britain and support for the ambition of eradicating it. Participants were engaged and even excited by the evidence that progress could be made, leading to support even from those participants who were initially the strongest 'poverty sceptics' to contribute *personally* towards tackling poverty, though not without attaching some important conditions.

2.1 What did people initially think about poverty?

- Low levels of awareness of poverty *and* of the government's pledge to end child poverty
- Denial of income poverty
- Tendency to attribute child poverty to bad parenting rather than a real lack of financial resources
- Lack of empathy with people living in poverty

(i) Low levels of awareness

Participants in the deliberative research conducted by MORI displayed very low levels of awareness of the existence of child poverty. People were initially much more comfortable associating child poverty with economically less developed countries than with the situation of children in this country:

> In England child poverty is more hidden away than if
> you're talking Sudan where you can see a kid of two or four
> standing there with an AK47 and weighing about two
> pounds. So it's more predominant and obvious…

Poverty at home in the UK did nevertheless have its own powerful set of associations:

Inner city, London streets, runaways, slums, big families, alcohol, drug abuse.

Nonetheless, there was considerable resistance from many participants to the idea that it is a significant problem in this country. The lack of initial awareness of poverty reported by MORI participants accords with low levels of public recognition of poverty amongst the British public reported by the Eurobarometer surveys. What is particularly striking about the Eurobarometer evidence, moreover, is the extent to which it reveals a gap between people's perception of the problem — as measured by the visibility of poverty in people's neighbourhood or local area — in this country and the actual prevalence of poverty in the UK. In 2001, visibility of poverty amongst UK respondents to the Eurobarometer survey was lower than in many countries including the Netherlands, France, and Belgium, all of which had significantly *lower* poverty rates than the UK, while in 1989 fewer UK respondents reported being aware of poverty in their local area than in any other country in Europe. The UK stands out among its European counterparts as having far lower levels of visibility of poverty than the actual (high) incidence of poverty would suggest. In addition, as we report further below, participants were also oblivious to the government's efforts to tackle child poverty in the UK.

(ii) Denial of income poverty

What the research revealed, moreover, was not simply low levels of awareness of poverty, but active resistance to the idea and in particular to the phenomenon of income poverty. Participants struggled to agree on what child poverty could really mean in an apparently affluent country like the UK, reaching instead for concepts like neglect and abuse.

I don't think income is a key factor for child poverty.

> You could be very poor financially but if your children are happy and you as a family unit are happy then it's not the same. It's neglect rather than financial.

> It's emotional poverty, where people are growing up in an emotional void.

At the heart of people's resistance to the idea of child poverty in this country seemed to be a sense that people can and should be comfortably well off. Generally high levels of affluence and economic security underpinned a perception of Britain as a rich country in which most people have more than enough to live on. The deliberative research participants, drawn from social classes B, C1 and C2 and living in the South East of England, were not themselves worried about their employment prospects, and described an economy which was functioning relatively predictably and successfully. There was, in addition, very little awareness of the existence of *in-work poverty* and of the difficulties in making ends meet even when people were working. The prevalent sense of economic affluence may also explain resistance to a definition of poverty purely in terms of income.

It may also be the case that people in relatively affluent positions are shielded from *seeing* the effects of poverty by the effect of a kind of informal residential segregation, with people who can afford to do so moving away from 'rough' areas where poverty is more prevalent.

(iii) Parents are frequently blamed for their children's poverty

Alongside widespread scepticism about the existence of income poverty, participants were strongly inclined to blame what poverty does exist on poor parenting:

> The UK equivalent [of third-world poverty] is poor upbringing.

There was little evidence of any kind of empathy with people in poverty, which manifested itself in participants' overwhelming tendency to attribute poverty to deficiencies of personal behaviour. Parents in poverty were repeatedly portrayed as wasteful, selfish and neglectful, to the detriment of their children:

> Again it's not fair to say single parent families but families that are hard up with money, you know, ultimately their child suffers … and if they're a selfish parent who wants to spend all their money on booze or going out then that's their fault.

> I think they just take drugs for escapism.

> It all goes on dog racing and scratch cards.

Parents who are 'hard up with money' were also viewed as deficient in the sense of being unwilling or incapable of investing time and interest in their children's development—despite the fact that those who were out of work would have more of their own time to do so:

> The non-working people don't have aspirations—they don't take interest in their child's education and yet they've got more time.

The idea that non-working parents lacked aspiration and motivation—for either themselves or their children—was a common theme, as was the belief that people in poverty are failing to take advantage of social or cultural opportunities, as opposed to simply not having the money to pay for basic services.

This tendency to attribute poverty to personal factors—the deficiencies in behaviour of 'poor' parents—is consistent with comparative survey data, which shows that people in the UK are more likely to prioritise behavioural causes of poverty—factors such as laziness or lack of will power—than most other countries in Europe. Comparative attitudinal data show that the 'laziness' explanation of poverty scored particularly highly for the UK in the mid seventies, with more than 44 per cent of British respondents choosing this explanation—a much higher proportion than in any other country in Europe (almost 15 per cent higher than the nearest country, Ireland).[iii] By the late eighties, the proportion of respondents attributing poverty to laziness or lack of willpower was noticeably lower, and had fallen still lower by 1993, though it has since increased again—a trend evident in many countries, including Germany, France and Belgium. In Britain, the 'laziness' explanation increased from a low of 12 per cent of respondents in 1993 to 22 per cent in 2001—which is nowhere near its 1976 high, but is still amongst the highest level in Europe (second only to Portugal, where the corresponding figure in 2001 was 27 per cent).

The number of respondents blaming poverty on personal failings such as laziness, as opposed to societal factors such as structural inequalities, varies over time, according to the wider socio-economic context. In most countries, including the UK, the numbers attributing poverty to injustice peaked in 1993, at a time of economic recession and high unemployment when respondents were presumably less inclined to regard those out of work as personally culpable for their situation. In looking at public beliefs about the causes of poverty, we therefore need to be aware of variations both in explanations over time, which reflect changes in the wider socio-economic climate, and also national differences, which appear to owe more to the particular political and historical context in each country. British respondents tend to be less convinced by 'unfairness' explanations of poverty than their counterparts in countries such as Spain and Portugal with similarly high incidences of poverty as Britain. The tendency in the UK to favour individual behavioural explanations over structural or social causes is particularly significant, as we shall see, because popular beliefs about the causes of poverty may affect people's attitudes towards the fairness of outcomes and the legitimacy of government intervention.

(iv) Lack of cultural reference points

Particular doubts were expressed about the existence of 'real' poverty amongst unemployed people living on benefits, with informal sources of information—most notably, 'social reality' TV programmes such as *Wife Swap*—being invoked by participants as 'evidence' of the comfortable, even luxurious, lifestyles of benefit claimants:

> I don't know much about the benefits system but from the sorts of programmes like *Wife Swap* when they swap wives … someone who earns … put them with a family who've got six kids and they say at the start the annual income is like 28 grand a year. Well, that's a hell of a lot of money that from benefits.

What is striking in this regard is that people's attitudes appeared to be shaped more by informal experiences and sources of information than formal sources of public knowledge or direct experience of life in poverty:

> The number of times you watch these documentaries on TV and you've got these families on there who has low income, got no money, almost guaranteed each one of them the parent or the parents will be sat there, fag …, probably a bottle of vodka, cheap vodka, they'd be drinking and smoking.

There was also a very strong belief that 'hard up' parents waste their money by gambling or drinking their income away.

The discussion therefore revealed a fundamental gap in public perception, with a lack of any cultural referents (in the form of *positive* role models) of people who are doing all they can for their families yet still struggling to make ends meet. It also revealed a fundamental lack of empathy with people living in poverty, who were seen as 'different from us'.

The instinctively negative and stereotypical views held by this group of relatively well-off people towards those in the lowest income groups reveals something of the way in which social and economic inequalities polarise and divide citizens – whether through physical separation (e.g. residential segregation) or through emotional *distancing* from people in poverty (a process of 'Othering').

2.2 The reality of poverty in the UK today

(i) What happened to child poverty in the 1980s and 1990s?

The proportion of children living in poverty (below 60 per cent of median income) rose steeply between 1979 and 1981, from 14 per cent to 20 per cent, and peaked twice at 32 per cent in 1993/4 and 33 per cent in 1996/7 (After Housing Costs). In 1979, 1 in 7 children lived in poverty. By 1998 the figure was 1 in 3. The progress made by Labour in reducing child poverty since it came into power has been impressive. In 2002/3, 3.6 million (29 per cent, AHC) children lived in low-income households. This represents a 15 per cent reduction (over half a million children) from a baseline of 4.2 million children in 1998/9. According to the Institute for Fiscal Studies the government is on track to meet the 2004/5 target of reducing the number of children in poverty by a quarter, but data for this period is not yet available.

Less progress has been made in reducing the proportion of children living in persistent poverty (below the poverty threshold in three or four years of a four-year period). Between 1996-99 and 1999–2002, this remained constant: 16 per cent of children remained in households living on incomes below 60 per cent of the median, and 26 per cent of children were below 70 per cent of the median in three of the previous four years.[iv]

As a consequence of reduced poverty levels, the government has also accomplished an increase in the living standards of low-income families between 1999 and 2001. Based on an index of hardship (comprising items such as housing conditions, essential items, health, and financial well-being), findings from the *Families and Children Study* (FACS)[v] show that in 1999, 41 per cent of out-of-work families were experiencing severe hardship. By 2001, this had decreased to 28 per cent among out-of-work lone parents and 22 per cent among the couples, with increased Income Support and Child Benefit rates since 1999 contributing towards this. During the same period, the proportion of children experiencing hardship fell from 67 to 53 per cent.

In 1998, the UK had the worst rate of child poverty in the European Union. By 2001 it had improved its ranking by four places, to 11th out of 15. The EU 15 countries can be grouped into three 'divisions' of performance in this regard. The UK has moved from the bottom to the top of the third division, which otherwise principally includes the Mediterranean countries. There is a significant gap between the UK and the next group, which includes most of the major Northern European countries including France and Germany. That group is again distinct from the highest performing group of Denmark, Finland and Sweden. Recent research by UNICEF indicates that the UK is unusual among the developed countries for the way in which it has 'significantly reduced its exceptionally high child poverty rate'.[vi] Yet despite the government's achievements the child poverty rate in the UK is still high by European standards and is a long, long way from its ultimate target.

This remarkable range of child poverty rates across Europe should immediately make us consider how far the outcomes in different countries are the result of different policy choices, and how far they are the result of other factors. The Commission—together with all those concerned about the continuing high level of child poverty in the UK despite recent progress—need to consider what must change over the next 15 years to bring our child poverty rate down to that of present day Denmark or Finland (which is now the government's declared goal).

(ii) What is the reality of life in poverty?

As we have seen, participants tended to blame the selfishness and waste-fulness of parents for what poverty does exist. One consequence of this view was that many assumed that parents could not be trusted to spend money on their children responsibly and so resisted the idea of increasing support through income transfers even when they did come to accept that deprivation exists and must be combated. Thus, while evidence of severe hardship and deprivation experienced by a small minority of children elicited the strongest reactions, a number of participants continued to insist that the appropriate response was to offer tokens for essential items (such as warm winter coats) rather than extra cash, which they thought would be frittered away.

The prevalence of this type of view — though by no means uniform amongst the participants, some of whom resolutely opposed the idea of food stamps or tokens — raises obvious problems for policy-makers and anti-poverty campaigners. The key point to be stressed is that participants generally had limited knowledge of the reality of life in poverty and that a high degree of misinformation existed about the behaviour and spending patterns of parents in poverty, which may be due to negative and stereotypical media images.

In fact, recent research in this area demonstrates the wholly inaccurate nature of common perceptions of parents' behaviour. Far from wasting their resources, as many MORI participants firmly believed, parents on low income spend additional income on their children's needs as a top priority. Research on levels of hardship in families by the Policy Studies Institute has examined whether increases in income for the lowest-income households since 1999 have resulted in improvements to living standards — and if so, where such improvements occurred, which means asking how the money was spent. While increases through taxation and benefits may have an impact on the absolute and relative measures of poverty, it does not mean an automatic improvement in children's stan-dard of living, if money is spent on inessential items or adults' personal consumption. The significance of the PSI's findings in this respect is that

25

it pinpoints where improvements occurred: as Alan Marsh observes, parents bought better food and clothes, had less debt and more heating. 'They did not', he states categorically, 'spend the money elsewhere'.[vii]

> I don't smoke, I don't drink, I don't go out, I don't eat meat. I have thought of getting rid of the TV, but I can't because it's for [my son] …There's absolutely nothing I spend my money on except just surviving, you know, paying bills and buying food. That's all I spend my money on.
> (Parent on Income Support)[viii]

A recent study examined the changes in expenditure patterns between 1996 and 2001 of families with children on essential items, particularly those related to the well-being and development of children.[ix] The aim of the research was to assess how the spending patterns of the poorest families responded to rises in real income arising from new work and welfare policy initiatives since Labour came into power. Such policies include Child and Working Families Tax Credits, New Deal for Lone Parents, and increases in Child Benefit and Income Support.

Compared with 1996/7, low-income families with children under the age of 5 experienced a 13 per cent increase in their income and an 11 per cent increase in their expenditure by 2001. The corresponding figures for high-income families with young children were 5 per cent for both income and expenditure. In contrast, low-income families with children aged 10+ experienced a smaller relative increase in income compared with higher-income families.

The MORI research highlighted the common public misperception that extra income is not spent with the interests of children as a priority, in particular on alcohol and tobacco. The Gregg findings, however, starkly demonstrate the opposite to be true. Between 1996/7 and 2000/1, as the income of poor families increased they spent relatively more on essential items such as food, clothing, and household goods and services. Expenditure on alcohol and tobacco by low-income families declined by over 8 percent—twice the rate of decline of higher-income groups.

With regard to child-specific expenditure, by 2000/1, poor parents spent disproportionately more on items beneficial to their children's well-being (for example, toys, games, books, clothes) relative to the most affluent families. The data show that for the highest-income families, spending on these items actually declined. For example, among families with children under the age of five, expenditure on children's clothing and footwear increased by more than a third for low-income families in contrast to a 17 per cent decline for the most affluent. The greatest increases in children's expenditure occurred in poor families where the youngest child was under the age of 5, as compared to poor families where the youngest child was 10+, which reflects the relative differences in income gains for these groups.

As well as seriously underestimating the extent to which parents in poverty use extra income to meet the basic needs of their families, the MORI participants did not recognise the impact that poverty has on parents. There is strong evidence to show that parents in poverty frequently sacrifice their own needs and well-being in order to protect their children from the effects of low income and hardship and to ensure that they come first. Findings from the Small Fortunes Survey, for example, highlight the extent to which parents go without necessities to provide for their children.[x] Large numbers of mothers reported that they went without clothes and shoes, holidays and entertainment. As many as one mother in twenty sometimes went without food to meet the needs of their child. Lone mothers on Income Support, in particular, reported making sacrifices: they were 14 times more likely to go without food, and over three times more likely to go without a holiday than mothers in two parent families not on Income Support.

> I think you have to give your kid a bit of money and a bit of
> enjoyment. As they get older, they are going to scrimp and
> save and look after their own kids. You go without yourself

to give to them don't you.[xi]

Mothers, in particular, employ a plethora of strategies for maximising household resources and stretching them as far as possible. They often prioritise and juggle spending between essential household bills, food and clothes for the entire family, which can lead to higher levels of worry and stress when trying to make ends meet. The cost can often be to their own mental and physical health:

> When they turned the water tap off, I felt very upset, I can't explain ... I feel very ashamed at that time. I feel personally ashamed. I feel ashamed at myself. I couldn't manage to pay the water and the supply had been cut off.[xii]

Where debts accumulate, usually when there is a delay in paying household bills or due to a sudden change in the financial circumstances of the family, low-income parents often cut down on essential spending in order to meet repayment demands, deal with harsh debt recovery practices from informal credit arrangements, or the threat of disconnection from utilities. Alongside this is the sense of guilt, shame, and personal responsibility associated with poverty and debt. Struggling on, and managing, a sparse income on behalf of family members therefore not only affects the material, psychological, and physical well-being of parents, but can also make the task of parenting much harder.

Contrary to the dominant assumptions of the MORI participants, the vast majority of parents in poverty see bringing up their children as the most important role in life, but nonetheless feel undermined in their ability to carry out that role due to the paucity of resources at their disposal. Of course there are examples of bad parenting in poor families, as there are in affluent families, and examples of outstanding parenting in very difficult material circumstances. However, as David Utting put it in 1995: 'Living on low income in a rundown neighbourhood does not make it impossible to be the affectionate, authoritative parent of healthy, sociable children. But it does, undeniably, make it more difficult.[xiii]

The difficulty remains that generalised misperceptions of the behaviour of 'poor' people are commonplace, possibly because those who hold these beliefs do not see the reality of life in poverty with their own eyes. Another possible explanation is that widespread ignorance is the result of a popular culture that shows the poor only as grotesque caricatures, and news media that constantly deny the reality of poverty. The Child Poverty Action Group publication, *Poverty first hand: poor people speak for themselves*, provides numerous examples of negative stereotypes of 'poor' people in the media — as lacking initiative and budgeting skills, as fraudulent 'professional' beggars, as single mothers who contrive to become pregnant only to 'jump the housing list', and as members of an 'underclass' characterized by 'drugs, casual violence, petty crime, illegitimate children, homelessness, work avoidance and contempt for conventional values' (Beresford *et al*, 1999, p. 137). Certainly, references to programmes such as *Wife Swap* by the MORI participants indicate that people's attitudes towards poverty are distorted by misinformation of this kind.

2.3 How do people respond to the evidence of the reality of poverty?

If people's initial (and deep-seated) instincts and beliefs about people in poverty represent the 'bad news' about public attitudes, the 'good news' is that certain kinds of stimulus had a powerful impact on people's views.

As we have seen, a striking finding of the research was the extent to which 'non poor' members of the public have a limited understanding of the impact of poverty on people's lives and a negative stereotypical view of the behaviour of 'poor' parents. An important advantage of the deliberative research format was that it allowed us to address some common misconceptions by presenting evidence of the extent and scale of the problem to our 'poverty sceptics'. Another useful feature of the format was that it allowed us to explore what kinds of arguments and sources of information appeared to have most impact in engaging people with the reality of life in poverty. So how did participants respond to evidence of the reality of life in poverty?

- Focusing on severe hardship and material deprivation has greatest effect on levels of engagement
- Surprise and approval of the boldness of the government's vision and the success of its approach so far
- Willingness to countenance higher taxes and redistribution to combat poverty and disadvantage

(i) Even 'poverty sceptics' are moved by evidence of severe hardship and deprivation, while they find technical measures confusing

It was the stark evidence of deprivation and severe hardship—hard facts such as one in fifty children going without a warm winter coat and one in twenty five going without a birthday celebration[xiv]—which proved to be most effective in persuading all participants, including our strongest 'poverty sceptics', that there is real poverty in the UK today that must be addressed. These facts often elicited strong responses from those who had initially shown hostility to what they saw as a debased concept of poverty, too easily applied to those who lacked only the latest trainers or mobile phone.

> It's depressing, some of the things children go without.

> It brings it home that some of the children if they live in poor conditions can't go swimming once a month. It's something that I take for granted.

> I tend to think of extreme child poverty as third world skeletal children. That's not because I want to deny the situation at home ... but I wasn't aware of some of the shocking facts and figures that we've been presented with.

A striking feature of the research, therefore, was the power of the statistics on severe hardship and deprivation to move people. In contrast, they tended to be sceptical when presented with the statistics of the numbers in poverty. The more technical, statistical measures (e.g., 60 per cent of the median income), meanwhile, generated a degree of confusion and resistance — with one participant, for example, wondering how it was possible to achieve a lower level of relative poverty since, as he saw it, 'some people will always fall below 60 per cent of the median'. European comparisons were useful here in showing that the level of child poverty on this measure actually varies widely between countries, with very low levels of relative poverty in countries like Denmark and Finland (where the poverty rate is less than 10 per cent, when measured as 60 per cent of the median income, and less than 3 per cent, when measured as 50 per cent of the median income).

Comparative data was also powerful in challenging the belief that poverty is inevitable: e.g., charts showing that the progress made in reducing child poverty by the government has improved the UK's position in the European 'league table' of child poverty since 1998.

(ii) People expressed surprise at, and approval of, the boldness of the government's vision and were impressed by evidence of the success of its approach so far

None of the participants were aware of Tony Blair's historic pledge to end child poverty in a generation. There was also little awareness of the role of government in developing policy and strategy to tackle this area in recent years, though some participants had a somewhat confused sense of policies that it has introduced:

F ...because you can claim something, even if you're on
   a low income you can claim something. I can't remember
   what it's called.

M Child benefit

F Is it income support?

F   Family credit
F   Is it? yeah family credit, that's it.

Their response to hearing about the pledge and subsequent targets and policy approach was uniformly positive: there was genuine surprise and encouragement about the figures showing that child poverty was not intractable—that things could change and that government policy could make, and had made, a difference. Despite initial scepticism about the existence of a problem, a few of the younger participants in particular were strongly impressed by the simplicity and boldness of the goal:

It's quite exciting—not just alleviating some of the symptoms but taking the whole thing away.

One possible explanation of high levels of poverty scepticism is that people believe this is a problem the government has solved. Our research shows this cannot be the case, because the participants were unaware both of the scale of the problem and of the progress that had been made.

(iii) Willingness to countenance higher taxes

Participants in our deliberative session moved relatively quickly from being sceptical about the very existence of poverty in the UK to recognising it as an important issue to be addressed. The key triggers for this shift were information about material deprivation and evidence that the problem is not intractable. The extent of people's enthusiasm for the goal emerged at the end of the deliberative session, when participants were asked whether they would in principle be willing to contribute personally to the alleviation of poverty.

Having established that every participant would—in principle—be willing to accept an increase in their own income tax for this purpose, all the participants were asked to raise their hand, and to lower them again at the point at which they were no longer prepared to pay more. The result of this exercise was that every single member of the group — without exception — expressed in this way their willingness to pay £20 more per month, if they knew that the money would be spent effectively to address child poverty. The precise figure should not be given too much weight, but this equates to an increase in the basic rate of Income Tax of 2 per cent for someone earning £20,000 per year (which is approximately average earnings for a full time employee).

A handful of participants declared themselves to be willing to pay a higher figure — up to £50 extra a month. Such findings have to be treated with a degree of caution, of course, in recognition of the fact that a discussion workshop focused on child poverty and life chances is an artificial environment which is bound to raise the salience of the issues it addresses for those people taking part. But what is most striking, perhaps, is the fact that every person, even those who were the most pronounced and vocal poverty sceptics in the earlier sessions, were willing to countenance paying more themselves to support anti-poverty initiatives.

When it came to putting forward reasons for tackling child poverty, their instinctive focus was very much upon the child concerned and upon the idea that everyone should start off with the same level of basic needs met and with the same set of basic tools to carve out a place for themselves in life. The argument that there is no need for poverty also resonated.

In conclusion, while it is encouraging that people's initial resistance to the idea of income poverty was partly alleviated by the presentation of stark facts about severe hardship and deprivation, questions remain about the adequacy of a deprivation-oriented approach. In particular, the finding that it was the evidence of severe hardship that proved most effective in capturing people's imagination presents an important challenge for campaigners on poverty issues because it suggests that the public arguments about what poverty is have not been won. If people only care about the most deprived — about the one in fifty children without the most basic necessities rather than the one in four currently below the technical poverty line — then the government's poverty target becomes all the more difficult to meet. It will be an enormous challenge to reduce the proportion of children in the UK living below the poverty line—in households with less than 60 per cent of median income—to among the best in Europe. It will be almost impossible to do so if the majority of people *do not know what poverty means or why it matters.*

3 | Life chances and the politics of equality

In addition to investigating people's attitudes towards poverty, the deliberative research allowed us to explore whether different kinds of argument have resonance with members of the public. We tested participants' responses to a number of other concepts besides poverty, including fairness, social mobility and life chances. In addition to finding out *whether* people cared about child poverty and unequal life chances, we were also interested in exploring *why* they cared: i.e., whether concern was motivated primarily by sympathy for the child's experience of poverty, by consideration of the impact of poverty on children's future life chances, or by awareness of the wider social costs of poverty, such as crime. In practice, however, it turned out to be very difficult to separate participants' priorities in this way. All seemed important, but none was really compelling in the abstract.

The phrase 'life chances' was not initially familiar to any of the participants. When asked for their spontaneous reactions to the term, participants tended to focus on the factors which were important influences in their own lives and so made reference to the support of parents, friends and family, as well as highlighting the importance of personal drive and ambition (including the role of parents in fostering or transmitting positive attitudes and motivation). In the initial discussion, the term was associated with opportunities for individual success rather than the achievement of basic social goods.

Social mobility, meanwhile, had a strong connotation for our first group of *social climbing*. The prime example of social mobility for one participant was Catherine Zeta-Jones, which was greeted with general agreement from other participants. For many, the concept of social mobility elicited associations with ambition and aspiration (which for some was a more welcome attribute than for others), but also with a society stratified into classes, which was regarded with some hostility. The term itself was only familiar to one or two participants and for most it seemed to represent the rather detached language of sociology textbooks, economists and politicians.

What was striking here was the individualistic nature of people's responses: there was an overwhelming feeling amongst participants that individuals can choose the outcomes they want and pursue them without impediments, which may well reflect their own relatively affluent social positions (and the tendency, perhaps, for people who had a strong sense of their own achievement to be more vocal in this section of the discussion).

3.1 The reality of unequal life chances

Participants articulated a strongly individualistic view of individual development, emphasising behavioural rather than structural causes of poverty, while also tending to assume that individuals who *were* successful were responsible for that success. As such, they tended to underestimate both the obstacles faced by people in poverty and the nature of inequalities between people from different social backgrounds.

Contrary to the dominant view, the reality of the situation is one of systematic inequalities: children born into poverty have a higher chance of living in poverty as adults, with their children then suffering disadvantage in their turn. This is not to say that being born into poverty is an inevitable life sentence, of course, since there are many individuals who do achieve good outcomes despite childhood poverty. But this should not distract our attention from the overall picture of systematic and unfair inequalities.

As we see it, there is a very clear moral case for tackling child poverty and the unequal life chances of children in poverty, which is based on two distinct arguments. The first is that we are concerned about the experience of poverty in childhood and the ways in which the lives of children are blighted by this experience. The impact of these experiences is a matter of concern in and of itself, regardless of its long-term consequences and effects on their future outcomes. Ultimately, in adversely affecting the lives of children and adults who experience it, poverty denies people's basic human rights and so denies the equal worth of every citizen.

The second reason for addressing inequalities of life chances is that we are troubled about the disparity in outcomes faced by children from different social backgrounds. What troubles us about the marked disparities in the experiences and opportunities open to children of say, professionals on the one hand and unskilled manual workers on the other is the fact that children's life prospects are determined by contingencies of social fortune — a mere accident of birth. Our sense of unfairness arises from the belief that social origin is no less arbitrary a determinant of educational, occupational and other outcomes than discrimination on the grounds of skin colour or religious belief.

Life expectancy at birth and infant mortality rates are good indicators of the overall health of a nation. Both have improved dramatically throughout the 20th century, in both developing and economically advanced countries. However, these key health indicators are both strongly associated with social class in the UK, and class in turn is associated with income levels and status. Despite the general increase in life expectancy, differentials have widened over the past 30 years, and are more pronounced for males than females. In 1997-99 the social class gradient for males and females was 1.9 years and 0.4 years higher, respectively, than in 1972-76.[xv]

In 2001, the infant mortality rate of children born into managerial/professional backgrounds was twice (6.9 infant deaths per 1000 live births) that of children from managerial/professional backgrounds (3.6 infant deaths per 1000 live births). Since 1996-98 the rate of improvement in infant mortality has been three times faster for managerial and professional classes than for those in routine and semi-routine occupations.[xvi] The chances of children surviving to their first birthday have become more unequal over this period.

With regard to educational outcomes, and leaving aside arguments about the value of test scores, there has been a significant overall improvement in educational attainment. For example, the proportion of pupils achieving 5 GCSEs at Grade A* to C in England rose from 41 per cent in 1992/93 to 53 per cent in 2002/03. Once again, there are marked inequalities between social classes. In 2002, children from higher professional backgrounds were twice as likely as children with parents in routine occupations to achieve the benchmark grades.[xvii] Yet whilst the social class gradient in attainment has persisted over time, there has been a reduction in the degree of inequality over the past decade.[xviii] In 1991, children with parents in managerial/professional occupations were four times more likely to get good grades than children from unskilled manual backgrounds. In 2000, they were just over twice as likely to achieve this. School attainment is still dramatically unequal and dependent upon social class, but progress is being made in closing the gap.

Inequalities in educational outcomes are reflected across the educational spectrum. Participation in higher education in the United Kingdom has increased from 460,000 full-time students in 1970/71 to around 1.3 million in 2001/02. However, children from more affluent backgrounds have been the principal beneficiaries of this expansion. The participation of children from manual backgrounds in higher education increased from 11 per cent in 1991/92 to 19 per cent in 2001/02. At the same time, the participation of children from non-manual social classes rose from 35 per cent to 50 per cent.[xix] Not only do young people from lower socio-economic backgrounds remain significantly under-represented in higher education, but the rate at which their participation has increased has been much slower than for those born into more advantageous situations.

The current generation of children is also adversely affected by the highly unequal distribution of wealth, a situation made worse by the rapid growth of house prices. Between 1983 and 2003, the prices of properties in the current most expensive 25 areas (as defined at the district level from census data) have risen in value at least sevenfold. In contrast, prices have barely doubled in the 25 areas with the lowest prices. If the housing wealth of the wealthiest decile of families by area were shared out amongst their children, wealth per child would be £82,490, compared to £11,671 per child in the poorest decile.[xx] The privileged child not only has recourse to greater wealth through inheritance, but also through parental financial help in young adulthood, which will aid the purchase of property.

Childhood origins shape adult destination, and the multiple disadvantages associated with poverty and inequalities of various kinds permeate different aspects of current childhood. As a consequence, there are marked continuities in socio-economic circumstances both inter-generationally and across the life-course, i.e., from parent to child, and from childhood to adulthood.

It follows that while intervention in the early years is crucial for reducing inequalities, people also require support at all stages of their lives to alleviate the inter-linked effects of poverty. Longitudinal research[xxi] has demonstrated that the most pervasive childhood antecedents to disadvantage in young adulthood are educational test scores, childhood poverty, frequent school absences, contact with the police and low parental interest.[xxii] In addition, children who grow up in poverty are more likely to have lower self-esteem, believe that health is a matter of luck, play truant and expect to leave school at the age of 16.[xxiii]

3.2 How did people respond to evidence of systematic inequalities?

If initial scepticism about poverty, especially the denial of income poverty, gave way to general willingness to countenance personal contributions through taxation, what did we learn about public attitudes towards life chances? Following the presentation of evidence about the unequal life chances of children from different social backgrounds, a number of specific facts and figures were most commonly cited in subsequent discussion:

- the reduced life expectancy of those from poor backgrounds
- their increased risk of mental illness
- the increased incidence of traffic accidents
- marked income inequalities between different ethnic groups

The effect of this stimulus was to bring life chances much more into the more immediate and powerful realm of human rights—especially the right to avoid an untimely death—and away from the abstract world of public policy and social research with its jargon of possible 'outcomes' in a hypothetical future. Perhaps unsurprisingly, people responded more strongly to the concrete than the abstract. Suddenly the differences in life outcomes between different socio-economic groups became much starker. Some participants reported feeling very strongly affected by this thought:

> It's opened my eyes. I don't think child poverty is addressed enough especially by politicians, it's certainly opened my eyes. Just listening to people's opinions and the statistics. I haven't had a particularly wealthy background but I've been blinkered to it. It's been worth coming just to talk.

Exposure to stimulus material about life chances certainly helped tip participants' opinions towards explanations of outcomes based on childhood socialisation rather than innate characteristics (i.e., 'nurture' rather than 'nature'). However, there was an interesting difference in the way people addressed evidence about health inequalities as compared to educational inequalities, with the former seen as more engaging and more objectionable. In part this may be because participants were previously unaware of the extent of the gap in health inequalities between social classes and ethnic groups. It may also be that the participants felt that people were more individually responsible for their educational outcomes than for their health outcomes.

In fact, the life chances stimulus uncovered an ongoing contradiction in the beliefs of our participants. Whilst professing great faith in the transformative effect on people's lives of good nurturing families, people also maintained a strong deterministic and individualistic streak and cited the importance of personal drive and determination, as well as the sheer luck of the draw. The MORI participants simultaneously believed in the primacy of individual and internal explanations of success in life, but were not surprised by evidence of systematic inequalities linked to factors such as parental class status.

The participants' belief in nurture as an important explanation of success was well illustrated by an exercise where they were taken through the Feinstein study of early cognitive development. This famous study shows how a sample of children from poor families who are judged as highly developed by age two were, on average, overtaken by the age of six by children from rich families who showed less initial ability.[xxiv] When the findings were graphically illustrated for the participants, the general response was that they were *completely unremarkable* because they were so much to be expected. One participant in fact expressed his surprise that anyone would find the results surprising.

For him, as for others, the links between family background and educational outcome were almost unworthy of comment, because they were taken for granted: participants readily volunteered numerous suggestions of the ways in which parents pass on advantages to their children, by paying for private tutors for example, or moving to live in an area with better schools. This is not to say that participants necessarily condoned inequalities in educational outcomes; in fact subsequent discussion revealed that there was very little support in the room for the existence of an independent schools sector. However, this part of the workshop made it clear that the participants had a sophisticated set

Figure 3.1 The determinants of life chances across the life-course & inter-generationally.

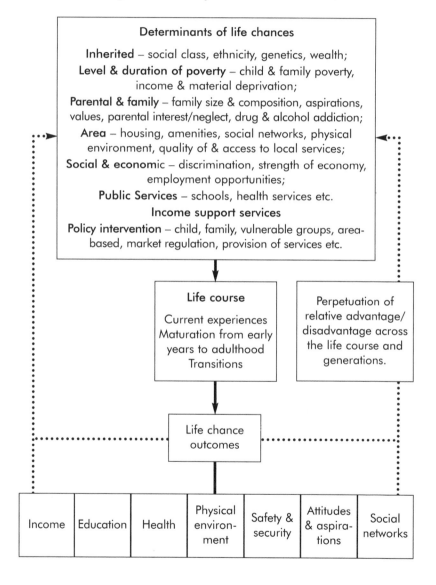

Determinants of life chances

Inherited – social class, ethnicity, genetics, wealth;
Level & duration of poverty – child & family poverty, income & material deprivation;
Parental & family – family size & composition, aspirations, values, parental interest/neglect, drug & alcohol addiction;
Area – housing, amenities, social networks, physical environment, quality of & access to local services;
Social & economic – discrimination, strength of economy, employment opportunities;
Public Services – schools, health services etc.

Income support services

Policy intervention – child, family, vulnerable groups, area-based, market regulation, provision of services etc.

Life course

Current experiences
Maturation from early years to adulthood
Transitions

Perpetuation of relative advantage/ disadvantage across the life course and generations.

Life chance outcomes

| Income | Education | Health | Physical environ-ment | Safety & security | Attitudes & aspira-tions | Social networks |

of sometimes contradictory attitudes towards the causes of inequalities in life chances.

A further effect of exposure to stimulus material and discussion of the causes of inequality was that the workshop participants began to recognise that government may have a legitimate role in addressing structural inequalities. In part this was about the major public services such as health and education, but it also generated a discussion about the role of government in relation to parents and the family. One strand of this discussion was specifically about bad parenting and the state's role in correcting this, but another strand of at least equal importance was about the challenges of parenting and the state's role in supporting and assisting parents more widely. There was little sense that the family in general was a private space from which the state should be excluded.

> The government can have an impact on what happens in the four walls of a household

Towards the end of the workshop, participants were asked about the possibility of shifting the emphasis of public services more towards the disadvantaged to improve their life chances. There was quite strong resistance to shifting resources so as to improve public services for disadvantaged people if this were to result in a fall in the quality of public services for anyone else. Participants were, however, generally prepared to accept services improving more slowly for the more affluent as an acceptable trade off for more rapid improvement of services for the more disadvantaged. Once again, it is important to qualify these findings as from a small sample in an artificial environment. Bearing that in mind, after being given the evidence and arguments, the group was broadly prepared to see public services used to level up life chances and close the gap between the rich and the poor.

4 | Making the case for more equal life chances

Since 1999, the government has introduced a raft of measures designed to reduce the extent of child poverty, based on the principles of helping parents into work wherever possible and providing extra financial support both for these families and for children whose parents are unable to work. These policies have been broadly successful, and there is general agreement that the government is likely to meet its first child poverty target of reducing the number of children living below the poverty line by a quarter—approximately one million children—by 2004/5, five years after the original pledge.

Does this progress so far mean that the government should simply continue with its current policies? There are several reasons why the answer is no. The first is that, even on the preliminary measure of child poverty as 60 per cent of median household income, the scale of the task is too big for the existing policy instruments alone to achieve. It is becoming increasingly apparent that welfare to work policies alone are not sufficient: one estimate is that either 70 per cent of lone parents with the youngest children or 100 per cent of those with older children would need to be in employment to achieve the 20 year target.[xxv]

Perhaps the most important reason why the government should not simply continue with its current approach is that an exclusive focus on child poverty is too narrow because it leaves out key concerns about broader divisions and inequalities. Critics to the left of the government have expressed the worry that beneath its laudable expressions of concern about child poverty, the government has shifted away from tackling deep-rooted inequalities in society. Tellingly, the experience of countries with very low rates of poverty indicates the very strong relationship between low levels of income poverty and a fairer distribution of income and wealth overall. It follows that it is extremely doubtful whether significant progress on reaching its child poverty targets can be sustained without a sea-change in its policy and political response to the problem. By focusing on the goal of more equal life chances for all children, the Commission intends in its future work to show the links between child poverty and broader divisions in society.

There is now strong evidence that relative social mobility in the UK fell in the late twentieth century: children born into manual worker families in 1958 had a better chance of entering higher occupations than children born into similar families in 1970. In other words, the relative chances of children from different backgrounds have become more unequal over time, with those born into affluent families retaining a stronger hold on their advantages.

Does the increasing strength of the link between family background and future outcomes mean that we should focus our attention on achieving the goal of *social mobility*? We argue that the concept of social mobility is unsuited to this task. On the one hand, if 'increasing social mobility' is simply a shorthand for improving the life chances of all disadvantaged children, then it may merely cause confusion, as this is not what many people understand by the term. If, on the other hand, it is narrowly about increasing the opportunities for gifted and aspiring individuals from 'poor' backgrounds to achieve their individual goals then it fails to capture most of what is important about creating a fairer society — and does nothing to counter the individualistic view of material success espoused by many MORI participants.

The aim must be to improve the life chances of all disadvantaged children, partly by increasing the value placed on 'lower' social positions and narrowing the gap in the experiences and outcomes of people in different social positions. The goal, in other words, is not simply to help talented children from the most disadvantaged backgrounds progress up a social ladder of opportunity, and so have access to higher quality services and public goods than their less-talented peers. Instead, we need to attend to the overall distribution of resources and opportunities and challenge the very existence of an exclusive and divided society, in which the accessibility and affordability of goods and services are largely determined by one's social position, and the relative rewards for different tasks and positions have often been influenced by those with most power and privilege.

Similarly, there are problems with the concept of meritocracy that lead us to eschew it as a guiding principle. At first glance, it is a simple matter of efficiency to want those with the most aptitude to fulfil the most challenging and responsible roles. But it does not follow that those with the highest marketable skills *deserve* the vastly inflated earnings that the highest paid now enjoy.

The badges of merit are strongly causally related to inherited advantages, as well as many other factors that should be irrelevant when it comes to allocating people to positions in society. There is a strong correlation between poverty and low educational attainment, and we are beginning to understand the causal mechanisms of this in finer detail. If merit were a basis of desert, but in its most easily demonstrable forms is also strongly causally related to family background, then it would appear that individuals deserve their advantages on the basis of their *parents'* characteristics. This offends against common sense. Similar arguments can be made about the many other factors that influence the ability of an individual to demonstrate merit—their race, gender, and place of birth to name a few. There may be good reasons to pay doctors more than cleaners, but desert on the basis of merit is not one of them. As our deliberative research participants suggested, we might also want to question how *much* more they should be paid if we are trying to create a fairer society.

What concerns us, in other words, is not merely the fact that talented children from income-poor backgrounds are less likely to realise their potential than those from affluent families, but that *all* children from income-poor backgrounds are less likely to realise their potential and to live in meaningful and rewarding ways than children from affluent families. The goal is therefore to improve the experiences and outcomes of all children and not merely to increase social mobility amongst the most able children, according to a meritocratic view of social justice.

4.1 Going public: meeting the public challenge

In this concluding section, we set out a strategy for 'going public' with the ambition to end child poverty, based on the following points:

- Raise the profile of the government's anti-poverty strategy amongst the wider public by making an explicit pledge to take the next million children out of poverty in the next five years
- Publicise recent government progress in this area far more widely and balance the moral case with appeals to self-interest
- Combat negative stereotypes and lack of empathy
- Recognise that good parenting is critical, but is undermined by inadequate resources

First and foremost, Labour will need to 'go public' and lead the debate about poverty and inequality if its 20 year strategy is to be politically sustainable. Political decisions need to be made about where public arguments can build on and 'go with the grain' of current opinion, and where it is important to challenge it because prevailing myths present barriers to change. While considerably more research on public attitudes in this area would be valuable we believe our new qualitative research offers some important pointers for an effective public and political strategy. However, each of these lessons also throw up some important dilemmas and issues for further debate.

(i) Raise the profile of the government's anti-poverty strategy

The low visibility of poverty and lack of awareness of a political strategy to combat poverty indicate the need for a concerted political effort to raise the public profile of the issue. Ending child poverty can and must be a central objective for Labour, just as it should be a priority for all progressive political parties. The government has already set itself the target of halving the number of children living in poverty (defined on an income basis) by 2010/11. Including an explicit pledge in its general election manifesto to lift the next million children out of poverty over the next five years would give a prominent public demonstration of its commitments to tackling poverty and inequality and would signal that it is willing to fight the election on this issue.

(ii) Publicise success so far and articulate the 'business case' for tackling poverty

Labour can make the case now, in a way it could not do in 1997, for tackling child poverty. It can also effectively challenge other political parties to match its ambitions, and expect to gain public support for doing so. The ambition to end child poverty is the government's best kept secret. Our participants were—without exception—unaware of it. Yet when told about it, and despite their initial misgivings about the true extent and nature of poverty, their reaction was strongly positive. They found it impressive that government and politicians should aim so high. They also felt that it was only right that an affluent country like the UK should be free of poverty. Perhaps most important, however, was their genuine surprise at evidence that child poverty is not inevitable and is not an intractable problem. International comparisons that show other European countries have very low poverty rates were one source of such evidence. Another was information about the government's success to date in taking a million children out of poverty. This was probably the single strongest factor in those shifts of opinion towards tackling poverty that took place during the deliberative session, and strongly suggests that the government should make much more of its success so far. It also supports the case for including an explicit pledge to take 'the next million children' out of poverty in Labour's General Election Manifesto. Placing the government's achievements and commitments with regard to child poverty higher on the political agenda could help to rekindle the public's faith in the efficacy of politics and politicians.

This sense of possibility also turned out to unlock another set of arguments. For if poverty really could be tackled, then it would be a shame, and wrong, not to do it. Participants now touched on aspects of what the Commission has called 'the business case' for tackling poverty – the waste and cost of not tackling poverty, and of storing up problems in terms of crime and anti-social behaviour. At this point, the discussion between participants revolved around the question of whether it was the business or the moral case for tackling poverty which was most compelling, rather than whether it was worth bothering with at all.

(iii) Combat negative stereotypes and lack of empathy with people in poverty

Perhaps the most important task for anti-poverty campaigners is to challenge the persistent myths and stereotypes about parents in poverty. Clear evidence exists of the actual consumption patterns of parents in poverty. Contrary to the expectations of many MORI participants, families in the lowest income groups, who have seen increases in their income since 1998, have spent less on personal commodities such as alcohol and cigarettes and disproportionately *more* on their children as a result. The findings of research demonstrating the inaccuracy of commonly held views needs to be disseminated and reported more widely. But if this is to be a dialogue with a broader public, rather than 'us' persuading 'them' of what we already think, anti-poverty campaigners will need to consider how they respond to the kinds of concerns raised by participants in the MORI study.

The government, for its part, needs to dispel pernicious myths about the poor, not least because the perpetuation of mistaken beliefs about

49

the behaviour of parents in poverty will obstruct progress towards its own anti-poverty objectives. Part of this is being more careful about its own language.

The 'rights and responsibilities' approach adopted by the government chimed with many members of the public. But, by 'starting from where the public are' there is a clear danger that myths and stereotypes are not challenged, and are in fact reinforced. The government must undertake to lead public debate in this area, rather than wooing a sceptical public or simply pandering to misinformed beliefs and judgements. Rhetoric about supporting 'hard working families' resonated with many of our participants. However, because they did not believe that anyone working hard could be poor, they also believed that the poor could not be working hard. 'Hard working families' readily becomes therefore a counterpart to negative stereotypes of lazy, non-working, poor families. Furthermore, given that comparative data shows that the British public has traditionally been rather more punitive in its attitudes towards people in poverty than their European counterparts, it is even more important for the government to take a lead on this issue in the UK than elsewhere.

(iv) Recognise that good parenting is critical, but is undermined by inadequate resources

Our participants all saw good parenting as critical to children's life chances. Most believed that a good parent, even with minimal financial resources, can provide their children with a good start in life. Few accepted that lack of material resources make it more difficult to be a good parent. At the same time our workshop participants recognised that parenting was a challenging task for all families, and that there was a legitimate role for government in supporting them in this task.

If we are concerned with building support for interventions aimed at supporting poor families in particular, this suggests that politicians and anti-poverty campaigners need to highlight the evidence that mothers and fathers struggle to be good parents to their children despite the difficulties of their circumstances. They also need to demonstrate how good parenting is not usually enough to overcome the hurdles poverty places in the way of children. As Michael Rutter (1974) famously expressed it: 'Good parenting requires certain permitting circumstances. There must be the necessary life opportunities and facilities. Where these are lacking even the best parents may find it difficult to exercise their skills'.[xxvii]

Part Three

The Fabian Life Chances Lectures

5 | David Miliband
'A fairer Britain'

The Fabian Commission on Life Chances and Child Poverty is important. It addresses the heart of politics. Where you are born has more impact on your life chances in this country than in most other countries. Our mission as a party and a government is to change that — to liberate talent and discover potential by tackling hardship and extending opportunity. A fairer Britain making for a better Britain. So it is right that subsequent lectures in this Fabian series will look in detail at different aspects of national life: health, education and community life.

Today I want to stand back and address the wider context. As we look towards the manifesto and an election campaign, we need to make an argument to the British people, and not just an offer. My argument today is as follows:

• First, that the politics of life chances is the politics of extending the good things in life; it is about equality when it comes to rights, inclusion when it comes to opportunities, and mobility when it comes to rewards; in other words it is the core of political economy in advanced industrialised countries; and in our country there is good cause for grievance — inequality in life chances defines the moral, economic and social agenda we face. Address it and we address the concerns of voters and the needs of the country.

• Second, that the coming election will decide whether we can entrench a modernised social democratic approach to life chances at the heart of our politics. We have proven competence in the first term; we have delivered progress in the second; a third term will decide whether this is a realigning government.

• Third, that New Labour is immeasurably stronger — in ideological and intellectual terms — in addressing these issues and achieving this realignment than it was ten years ago. Our vision and values retain popular support; and there is a distinctive, effective and progressive set of big ideas about how to extend life chances — in employment, in public services, in civic society — that we should be proud to defend, develop and extend.

• Finally, that we must understand exactly the Conservative strategy. They have policies based on the verities of the 1980s; but they have for the moment abandoned discussion of them. At a time when we can be increasingly confident of the power and relevance of our ideas, they are increasingly worried about the political consequences of theirs. Their strategy instead is to change the subject, to any other subject in the newspaper headlines. It is Thatcherism wrapped in opportunism. Those of us who care about the politics of life chances have to make our definition of the condition of Britain — the story of opportunities yet to be extended — the centrepiece of the election. The battle of ideas can only be won if it is ideas that are being discussed.

The Politics of Life Chances

The purpose of Labour politics is to bring the life chances of the most fortunate in our society within the grasp of all the people, rather than just a privileged few. It is simple, not complicated, to describe: for reasons of morality but also efficiency, we believe that opportunity and security, the foundations of freedom, should be extended as far as possible, to as many people as possible. That means in education, in employment, in housing, in public services and in retirement our responsibility is to use the power of collective action, not only through the state, to advance the freedom — real freedom — of the individual. Three dimensions seem to me to be key:

- Life chances depend on social equality. Where there is discrimination, for example on grounds of gender, or race or religion, there can be no equality of life chances.
- Life chances depend on social, economic and political inclusion. Where individuals or groups exist outside the mainstream of society — excluded from employment or housing or pensions, or excluded from the opportunities and support necessary for employment or housing or pensions, or excluded from the political process — then life chances are violated.
- And life chances depend on social mobility. Unless people can get on, and have the means to get on, then the best chances in life are restricted to those who already have them. Individuals are worse off; the country is worse off.

The necessity of such action is not new. It motivated the Liberal government of 1906 and the Labour government of 1945. In our own time, the economic argument for maximising life chances not just of some but of all is compelling: every talent wasted is lost to the individual and lost to the country.

I believe there is good reason to be proud of genuine progress in the last eight years. I will explain what I mean in a moment. But although we should be proud, we should not be satisfied. Our pride in progress should whet our appetite and renew our commitment to do more, because the evidence is that our country remains deeply scarred by unequal life-chances:

- When it comes to social equality, the pay gap between men and women and for certain ethnic minorities is stubbornly high.
- When it comes to social inclusion, the educational outcomes of children in the middle are lower than those at the top, and of the

unemployed are five times worse than those of the employed.
- And when it comes to social mobility, in one study the chances of the son or daughter of someone in social class V reaching social class I are 32 times lower than the chances of the son or daughter of someone in social class I staying there.

These figures are not the fault of one government. They have built up over generations. And our job is to roll them back over generations.

Three Phases of New Labour

This is the context for an assessment of New Labour's performance in government since 1997, and the prospects for the future. In 1997 we had a lot to prove. It was not just our party that was on trial, but our way of thinking.

In the course of the 1960s, the governing nostrums of pragmatic social democracy — the movement that had built the post-war welfare state — came under assault from the left. In the 1970s and 1980s, the assault came, more effectively, from the right. Their claim was simple but also stunning: everything we believed, and everything that previous, moderate Conservative governments had believed, about how to run the economy and achieve social change, was wrong. The crux of their argument was that government was the problem not the solution, the source of post-war decline, not its remedy.

This meant that in 1997 the first Labour government for 18 years faced particular tests. I would describe them as follows. First, whether we were competent in the basics of running a modern, advanced industrialised economy; second, whether we had the insights and determination to take on more complex policy tasks; and third, whether we had the ability to reshape the political agenda. At each stage we were confronted with the question of whether we had a modern and relevant understanding of the relationship between increasingly global markets, increasingly active civil society, and government increasingly stretched to address new needs.

The first phase involved exorcising the demons of the 1980s and early 1990s. I don't just mean the ritual international humiliations of the ERM and the Beef War: I mean the people working for £1.50 an hour; the annual winter crisis in the NHS, and the weekly discussion of 'trolley waits'; the descent to 42nd in the world education league, with outside toilets as the symbol of an education system locked in the nineteenth never mind the twenty-first century; the more than one million children living in poverty; the one in five households with no one working.

For 18 years these had been presented as facts of life — maybe distasteful, maybe cruel, but essential and integral to the smooth functioning of a market economy. After all, the fall of the Berlin Wall had proved that there was no alternative. Or so it was alleged.

We had to slay these Tory demons. And in the process we had also to slay demons of our own — on the economy, on crime, on international alliances. All of this had to be tackled to establish the viability of an alternative to Conservative government.

Some people say we went too slowly. I prefer to believe that we moved with deliberation, our eye on the long game. After all it had taken 100 years to legislate for the first minimum wage and to enact constitutional reform. But people were impatient for change, and my argument for gradualism only holds if we turn the first steps into solid foundations for longer term change. That is what I believe we have been doing since 2001.

The second phase of the government has consumed this Parliament. It has taken hard administration for very clear purpose — to extend life chances for people denied them:

- The New Deals have helped 1.2 million of the hardest-to-reach people into employment
- Waiting lists are tumbling, with the elimination of the longest waits, as capacity is built in and out of hospital
- School exam results in inner city areas are rising faster than the national average; that is the product not of one policy but many,

from teacher recruitment and training to out of school support

- Tackling anti social behaviour is an important part of the drive to extend life-chances; it was not featured in the 1997 manifesto, yet today there are 4600 community support officers, more than 3000 ASBOs and 57000 Fixed Penalty Notices bringing order to communities

- The seemingly inexorable rise in child and pensioner poverty, a key driver of life chances, has been arrested and reversed, early intervention established as a core principle of policy in the creation and expansion of Sure Start around the country, and on perhaps the most difficult indicator for government, the growth of income inequality has been arrested.

We should make no apology for engaging in the hard slog of administrative reform. That is what government is about. What we need now to do is defend its results, and link the administration and the results to our bigger purpose — of reshaping the political agenda around our values. That is our opportunity in the election campaign and our responsibility in a third Labour term.

Our challenge at the next election, whenever it is, is to win a mandate to entrench a new settlement in British politics. In the same way that after the 1980s, no government will contemplate the abandonment of fiscal caution, the nationalisation of competitive parts of the economy, or a return to strikes without ballots, so we have our own set of truths that we want to make an enduring part of the country's politics.

The truth that an active welfare state can cut unemployment, change the composition of public spending and attack poverty; the truth that tax-based universal services are the right basis to develop specialist services to meet diverse needs; the truth that fair treatment at work — for employees, for parents — is part of a flexible economy not its antithesis; the truth that power devolved is politics enhanced; the truth that public investment in transport, in research and development, in science is essential to the wealth-creating base; the truth also, and at a tangent to the argument today but important nonetheless, that Britain's best interests are served in the European Union not outside.

These are the planks of a modernised social democratic Britain; they form the agenda we are setting not the agenda we inherited; and they are at the heart of our constitutional purpose to put power, wealth and opportunity in the hands of the many not the few. We wrote those words because we believed them, and they are at stake in the battle for a third Labour term.

Building a Social Democratic Settlement

My contention is that at this election our chance is to entrench these truths in our national life, and that we are ready to do so because of the process of modernisation that we have undertaken. The last ten years have made us stronger not weaker — above all stronger ideologically and intellectually. I say this for four reasons.

First, since 1997, we have seen key policies work. As we developed policy for government, as we did research on what worked, we thought we had developed workable policies. But we could not know. We believed the minimum wage could raise wages without costing jobs; we believed devolution could strengthen the UK; we believed in the National Literacy and Numeracy Strategy; but we couldn't prove any of these things were true until we did them. Well now we can draw confidence from the results.

Second, we have a richer and wider and deeper policy agenda for the third term than we had for the first. This has been the success of the five year plans, and the detailed work within the party through the Big Conversation and the Warwick process. Across government, legislative and administrative changes have been laid out. People can disagree with them, but no one can be in any doubt about what a third term Labour government would do.

Third, we have a better understanding of the changes in the outside world, and how we measure up to them. The two strategic audits of the UK have given us a clear picture of where we stand, what is world class, and what we can do to match it. We know that successful people, communities and countries use knowledge to generate wealth, are flexible in the face of change, are networked globally and locally. That is our ambition for Britain and the British people.

Finally, the British people have maintained their commitment to our values and vision, even when they are frustrated about delivery or what they perceive to be distractions. The contrast with the 1980s is clear. The majority of the public never warmed to New Right values; they voted for Mrs Thatcher because they saw no alternative. But the public still want to believe in us.

For these reasons I believe we have gained strength. We have lost some friends through our decisions. That is what happens in government. But my argument is that we now have a sharper, clearer view of what constitutes a viable social democratic strategy for the twenty-first century. It is a new approach; it has involved rethinking; it does involve tough choices. But while we do not have all the answers we have shown that there is a way to combine dynamic markets, enabling government and empowered communities to extend life chances.

Instead of majority values and progressive ends being in conflict, they are aligned.

The economic strategy of Bank of England independence, fiscal prudence and promoting competition has kept down interest rates and inflation and driven up growth. In the next Parliament there will be practical steps to take these changes further, for example reform of planning, streamlining of inspections and regulation, deepening of the skills base.

The welfare strategy of making activity and independence the focus of policy is helping to change lives. Welfare to work, direct payments to disabled people, integration of tax and benefits for families and pensioners are all putting the empowerment, support and reward of citizens at the heart of policy. In the next Parliament we have set out how we want to go further, in childcare, in reform of Incapacity Benefit.

The strategy of using diverse and flexible services to offer specialised provision in public services is helping to change lives. We keep the

61

commitment to tax-funded services free at the point of use; we modernise delivery mechanisms to tune those services to individual need; we reform staffing structures to make more of the public service ethos; we use alternative providers to drive innovation, expand capacity and replace under-performance. In the next Parliament we take the next steps, for example to modernise health care for those with chronic conditions, or to create the organisational flexibility to tune education to pupil need.

The strategy of community empowerment, nascent in some areas but developed in others, is helping to promote collective solutions, some rooted in the renewal of local government, some rooted in city-wide coalitions for urban renaissance, some rooted in civic society and the voluntary sector, in partnership with the state rather than run by the state. There are plans to go further—for example with power devolved to neighbourhoods in key areas relating to the local environment.

There is no substitute for ideas in politics. These ideas are the foundations of a different kind of progressive politics, with the capacity to set the tramlines for policy for many years to come. They are the battle hymns of social and economic change. And they provide a stark contrast to the Tories.

Turning Ideas into Votes

Speaking to the 1987 Scottish Conservative Party conference, shortly before the 1987 election, Nigel Lawson gave a speech in which he argued that Conservative dominance was rooted in ideas. He said: 'No British government has ever been defeated unless and until the tide of ideas has turned against it. And far from turning, the tide of ideas which swept us into office in 1979 is flowing even more strongly today.'

Today, I believe that the Conservatives fear the tide of ideas. They had a choice after the last election: to make one last push for Thatcherism, or to move on. They decided on one last push. Their policies have not moved on from the 1980s: cut public spending, abandon active labour market policy, introduce subsidies for those going private in health and education.

But since January, something has changed. Not their platform: it is hard right. Yet they will do anything not to debate it. I believe the reasoning is clear.

They have assessed their chances of winning an argument about whether the state should spend 42 per cent of national income or 40 per cent; about whether public money should be spent first on those people who can already afford private health and education services; about whether they have effective plans for the economy, for housing, for employment; about whether it is the responsibility of government to lead the fight against poverty. And they have decided that the last thing they should be doing is having an argument about these things.

That is why we had the farcical situation last week of quotations from Conservative spokesmen being described as Labour lies; of a Conservative candidate deselected because he said in public about public spending what is only meant to be whispered in private; and on Monday the ultimate humiliation for a right-of-centre political party: the publication of the economic chapter of their manifesto smuggled out between announcements on travellers and GM foods. This is the party that used to run on the economy; now they are running away from the economy.

Thatcherism is now wrapped in opportunism. They don't think they can win an argument about the core issues of economy and public services that have traditionally divided the parties. So they aim to ride the headlines not solve the grievances: from licensing to asylum they actually have no solutions.

Our ambition is that the Conservatives do adapt to the new contours of policy that we have set out. But they have not done so yet. We know only have succeeded when in every party manifesto there is a commitment to seek the abolition of child poverty—and an argument about how to achieve it; a commitment in every manifesto to tackle health inequalities—and an argument about how to achieve it; a commitment in every manifesto to extend life chances in education, employment and housing—and an argument about how to achieve it. But they have not acquiesced yet. Their agenda for government rejects our truths, puts our progress under threat, and takes us back. That is why this election is important.

The politics of life chances will be the focus of a third Labour term. The focus of more debate, more innovation, more action. But it will not even be on the agenda if we do not win. And to win, we need to make clear that the choice at the election, whenever it is, is fundamental. The stakes could not be higher, or the prize more enduring.

Response by Polly Toynbee

There is something poignant about re-reading David Miliband's speech now the election is over. At the time it seemed wonderfully optimistic and uplifting. I came away hoping this would be a better campaign than I had reason to expect after this ambitious outline for embedding a social democratic future steeped in ideas of social justice into national thinking. Now, after the election, there is a strong sense of a missed opportunity. Whatever the election was about, it was rarely if at all about the rousing sentiments expressed here.

Let me reprise what he said: 'We need to make an argument to the British people, not just an offer'. Did they? No, they made offers, like selling goods to truculent buyers. 'A third term will decide whether this is a realigning government'. Well, there is nothing in the Queen's speech to suggest it is. Instead there is more of the old triangulating between good solid progressive policies and rightward appeasing gestures to throw the public off the scent. 'The battle of ideas can only be won if it is ideas that are being discussed' he said and he called for 'reshaping the political agenda around our values' Yes! But there was precious little of that to be found in Labour's campaign.

Because there was so little of this inspirational element, it would be difficult to claim that Labour had succeeded in the task Miliband set: 'Our challenge at the next election is to win a mandate to entrench a new settlement in British politics.' Sadly, Labour can hardly claim to have won a mandate for anything. With only 36 per cent of the vote and just 22 per cent of the electorate, the most they can claim after a lacklustre campaign is a grudging consent that they should carry on.

It is not that the public rejected the social justice idea Miliband puts so power-fully here. It is just that they were never asked, never invited to join the vision, never trusted to sign up to anything so ambitious. They were only trusted to vote out of self-interest: remember Alan Milburn's dismal and cynical early slogan: 'Your family better off'? It has been Tony Blair's failing all along never to believe that we have or could have a social democratic majority in the country.

From this election result, it looks as if he was wrong: all Labour's lost votes went to the Liberal Democrats, none to the Tories. The Tory proposition, such as it was, got not one new vote. The chances are, had Labour run a campaign modelled on David Miliband's proposition here, there would have been a rallying to the flag, despite Iraq. Even with Tony Blair still at the helm, despite his unpopularity, the whole tone of the election might have been turned into something better had he only dared make social justice and children's life chances the reason for voting Labour.

Sadly, there is a tendency among all these ministers to raise their game when they talk to the Fabians. Perhaps they feel free in the privacy of their own kind to express the views that propelled them into the Labour party in the first place. Perhaps they feel free of the constraints of Downing Street scrutiny or watchers from the Daily Mail. But the passions they express on equality and justice here so rarely emerge on television or radio, where it really matters. So we wait to see whether a future leadership will allow these thoughts freer reign in the outside world. Or will we have to wait for a younger generation—the Miliband/Cooper cohort—unscarred by the 18 wilderness years to feel liberated to speak out in these terms, even where the right wing press can hear them?

Polly Toynbee is a member of the Fabian Commission on Life Chances and Child Poverty and a columnist on the Guardian

6 | John Reid
'Aspiration moves the world'

I want to start with an assertion that I hope will be seen to become a truth as my argument develops. Over the last few years there has been something deeply patronising and unpleasant about the way in which sections of the left and the right have claimed that New Labour hasn't been about values; hasn't been about our passion for changing the world; has just been pragmatic; has just been electoral.

I want to demonstrate today that our belief in encouraging and meeting the modern aspirations of working people by developing plans to empower people by extending to them more information, more choice and more power over their own lives, is a belief driven strongly by left wing values and passion. And I want to explain how, if we can develop it properly, that power will increase life chances for those who have previously had them stunted.

Sadly, for some on the left the only real passion, the only proper radical value seems to be represented by building state institutions that tell people what to do. For them, 'proper left politics' is based upon the confiscation of significant sums of money from working people's wallets through taxation and creating public service institutions that tell working people which school they have to send their child to and which hospital their mum has to go to. Anything else they seem to believe isn't really principled, isn't really radical, because, well by definition, it's not telling people what to do.

This old thinking, progressive in the first half of the last century, now acts as a fetter on the development of truly personal services in the first half of this century. This ideology of the past, which is sometimes wrongly portrayed as the only policy that takes inequality seriously, is one that involves a strong state telling people what to do. Therefore, if you argue against a strong state telling people what to do, then, so the sloppy thinking goes, you are inevitably not bothering about inequality.

So, it is against this loud background noise of the politics of shouted instructions, that New Labour has tried to work with people where they are, rather than where others tell them they have to be, and as a consequence is caricatured as pragmatic and unprincipled.

It's interesting historically to find out how the left got to this false conclusion—how some left wing journalists can actually say that New Labour's stress on 'empowerment' of working people is in some way a dirty word which has no value or passion on the left.

The early Labour movement fully recognised the central role of self-advance, self-help and individual effort in social liberation as an essential corollary to the exercise of state power. However, faced with the scale of the ills of industrial capitalism in the first half of the last century, it was reliance on the latter—state action and power—which was increasingly emphasised at the expense of the former.

Both during and after the Second World War, the left brilliantly espoused a political economy of austerity and sacrifice in a centralised war-time state. But during the 1950's, as day to day wealth grew for working people, the left was unable to adapt to the realities of the emerging consumer society.

Those dimensions of self-expression and individual ambition and fulfilment—concomitants of economic and social progress—were not values that the 1950s Labour Party felt able to endorse. There was a mistaken belief that politics that sprang from people's aspiration could only come from the comfortable middle-class. And this guilt by association—middle-class people aspire, therefore the left is against it—sticks to the issue today.

So the argument goes like this. Because New Labour develops its policy based upon people's aspirations, such a policy must only talk to the middle-class and it must therefore 'sell out' the working-class.

This is patronising rubbish. It is historical fact that the history of the Labour movement, its institutions and its successes have developed only because of the aspirations of working people to better themselves and their families.

It is a historical fact that the politics of black improvement in our society has come about because of the sharp ambitions and aspirations of black men and women to better themselves and their families.

And if you want to be told exactly where to go, suggest to a woman that women's improvement or liberation has come about except through the active and day-to-day fight of women to improve their status in society. Of course we can collectively provide the opportunities by collectively providing resources. But, the defining characteristic of social change is the energy, effort, ambition and application of individuals themselves.

Individual aspiration and social movements of aspiration move the world.

Look around almost every Labour Party meeting. People have worked hard for themselves and their kids; the kids have worked hard at their schooling and their university. When they have the time, people work hard in developing their local community. All of this is about aspiration and ambition.

Some of this aspiration is about themselves as individuals and some of it is about the collective good of society. But it is this aspiration and ambition that drives the world forward and makes the left grow in influence.

But New Labour does not, nor should it, simply accept the distribution of aspiration as it exists at the moment. The point of our politics is to increase the aspiration of those people who have felt that they have no chance. The point of the left is to increase working people's aspirations and to provide support that meets those aspirations.

So when poorer people feel that public services are insufficiently responsive to their needs, what we do is encourage their aspiration, not tell them off for wanting more. Our third term will extend the work of our second, aspiration will find its way into even more parts of society where it has been lacking before.

Let me make it clear. The reduction of inequalities is a central issue to New Labour's philosophy and is a key part of what we are achieving and what we will achieve if we win a third term.

This statement only appears news-worthy at all because the media and some on the left have hitherto confused the relationship between means and ends. Since New Labour is radically reforming the way in which we deliver public services, improving and modernising them to enable them to meet the expectations of a more ambitious population, then it has been assumed that are not longer interested in reducing inequalities. Not true.

Political, social and economic equality only improves when previously disadvantaged people work to change their position in society. government and public services can and must assist this process, but people's own motivation is at the core of change. The centre of New Labour's political and philosophical approach is to increase the power that people have over their own lives and opportunities.

Labour market equality improves when a 47-year-old unemployed man goes through the hard work of completely retraining and getting a new job. Educational equality improves when the family of an 11-year-old supports them to do the hard work of improving the child's literacy. Health equality improves when a teenage single mother goes through the hard work of giving up smoking.

Now you can hear the parodying of this position. 'John Reid says the poor have only themselves to blame. It's all up to them and there is no responsibility for government.'

Nothing could be further from the truth. In all three of these cases the New Labour government has provided support to help develop people's motivation and to translate it into reality. With jobs, New Labour created

69

a stable economy and developed very specific policy offers with the New Deal which helped different groups of people to get into work. For improving literacy, New Labour provided better support in schools and very specific support for young children and their parents on learning literacy. And, for improving health inequalities New Labour has provided specific support with smoking cessation services.

Similarly, educational qualifications are a crucial issue in expanding life chances. New Labour introduced policies for the teaching of literacy and numeracy in primary schools. At the time, it was felt that 11-year-olds were being judged against a standard that would undermine the aspiration of previous underachievers.

It is interesting to look at the actual outcomes. One of the proxies used in education for poverty and inequality is whether the child receives free school meals. A school where less than 8 per cent of children receive free school meals would represent better-off parents. A school where over 50 per cent of them receive free school meals would represent a worse-off set of parents. If the first group of schools improve faster than the second group, then inequality gets worse. If the second poorer group of schools improve faster than the first then equality improves.

In 1997 there was a gap in Key Stage 2 English achievement between the better-off and the worse-off schools of 35 per cent. In the poorer schools fewer than half — 42 per cent — achieved the required level, with nearly twice as many in the better-off schools reaching that level. Over the 6 years from 1997 to 2003, both groups of schools improved, the better-off schools by 8 per cent and the poorer schools by 17 per cent.

So between 1997 and 2003 it's not just the fact that more 11 year olds can read and write, but that children from poorer schools are improving at twice the rate than children from better-off schools. In maths the rate of improvement of the poorer schools is nearly three times that of the better-off schools and in science it is two and a half times better. New Labour's literacy and numeracy hours have reduced educational inequality. They have done so by assisting pupils in schools with poorer backgrounds to develop their motivation to learn.

What does this mean for improving life chances in any Labour third term?

First, we must specifically and in detail try to increase the aspirations and ambitions of those whose ambition has been previously ignored or crushed. This cannot be done by general appeals to betterment, but by hard, specific work with communities and excluded groups. People who are disadvantaged are not 'all the same'. They are specifically disadvantaged and have made specific and personal attempts to improve their lives. The causes of disadvantage might be class, gender or ethnicity—big issues with big histories behind them. But the experience of disadvantage is specific. People who are better-off, with more money, education or better health, may well expect to be treated as individuals. But so do poorer people. And ultimately the only services that will reduce inequalities are ones that treat them more personally.

In health, for example, this has meant finding out exactly what, for example, middle-age, working-class men might worry about with smoking. It also means finding out why different women, from different classes and in different circumstances are left battling with depression. They are not all the same.

So, firstly, this puts the personalisation and choice agenda at the core of the policies to reduce inequalities. This may appear novel, but in fact it is merely the contemporary re-assertion of our traditional values.

Last year to some consternation I quoted RH Tawney on this issue. He said: 'But equality of provision is not identity of provision. It is to be achieved, not by treating different needs the same way, but by devoting equal care to ensuring that they are met in the different ways most appropriate to them, as is done by a doctor who prescribes different regimens for different constitutions, or a teacher who develops different types of intelligence by different curricula'. In one sentence arguing for personalisation, written 75 years ago, Tawney prefigures what should be central to New Labour's third term philosophy.

Secondly, our future policies must recognise the centrality of empowerment. Getting a job improves the amount of power a previously unemployed person has over their life. Learning to read and write improves the amount of power people have over their lives. Choosing the time you go for a hospital appointment and the choosing the doctor you see, gives you power over your life; and, yes, giving up smoking gives you power over your life. Government policies to reduce inequality must give you more power over your life.

The government that achieves this will enable people and not instruct them. In fact the government that merely tends to instruct working people takes away from their power and reduces their capacity.

So policies need to be personal to work with people as they are and not as a uniform unit of the public. Policies need to empower people and not tell people what to do.

And above all policies need to recognise that power lies in increasing aspiration and motivation. If public services treat people as if they are units of the public, they will fail to engage with the very specific way in which people become motivated to improve. If we fail to develop their power over any aspect of policy, then we will not increase their motivational capacity.

So, for me the third term will turn quantity into quality; it will continue to unlock people's aspirations; will continue to empower working people in new ways and will therefore continue to transform British society, precisely because it recognises and plays to the simple fact that it is the ambition and drive of ordinary people which is the greatest dynamo of change and improvement.

Response by Victor Adebowale

I welcome John Reid's commitment in this lecture to the principle of life chances, and his focus on reform of our health services. In many ways, health is the single most important factor in determining life chances. At the end of the day, if you've got no life, you've got no chances. And because the impacts of individual ill health are felt throughout families and communities, improving individual outcomes has wider benefits.

As John Reid says, there are still too many people in this country whose aspirations are thwarted by the system. And there are still too many people who don't even dare to have aspirations, whose chances are blighted at the very outset by poverty and deprivation. I applaud this government's emphasis on tackling these big inequalities. But there's been less progress so far in closing the gap in health outcomes than in education. In fact, there hasn't been much progress at all.

Whilst the social-class gradient in GCSE attainment has been reduced, inequalities between different social groups in rates of infant mortality and life expectancy have actually been increasing over recent years. A child from a poorer background has a higher chance of dying early and living a shorter life than a child from a more privileged background.

There's still an 'inverse care law' in this country, where the people who need most help are on the receiving end of the worst services. The latest figures published in the *British Medical Journal*, based on research conducted at Bristol University, show that the difference in life expectancy between men living in Glasgow City (with the lowest life expectancy) and Dorset East (with the highest) has risen to 11 years. This disappointing lack of progress means that the government is unlikely to meet its own national target to raise life expectancy in the most disadvantaged areas faster than elsewhere by 2010. It's time to make a concerted effort to reach out to the worst-off members of society.

It's important not to get too distracted by talking about 'choice' and 'personalisation'—ideas which appeal to the middle classes but don't much interest the people at the bottom of the pile, the people who just want some decent services, and don't have the time or money to go in search of them. First of all, we've got to close the inequality gap, if choice is going to be the key characteristic of Labour's third term health agenda.

And we've got to make the business case as well, appealing to the enlightened self-interest of employers and citizens who can see the costs of failure, in terms of both treatment and economic activity.

The resources of our health services have already increased dramatically, but, as John Reid says, we've got to work hard now to turn that quantity into quality, especially for the poorest. Tackling uneven life chances in health is going to be expensive, but we can't afford not to do it. In order for the government to make progress it's going to have to focus on bespoke social care solutions for the worst areas with the poorest people, and will need to really engage the not for profit sector in the creation of a trusted bridge, giving the poorest members of our society access to life improving services.

Lord Victor Adebowale is Chair of the Fabian Commission on Life Chances and Child Poverty and Chief Executive of Turning Point

7 | Alan Milburn
'Labour values'

I want to set out today what I believe to be Labour's purpose for a third term in government. I want to do so in a way that goes beyond the hurly-burly of the day-to-day election campaign. I want to set out our prospectus for what I will call the progressive modernisation of Britain, where opportunity is extended from the few to the many.

In any election campaign it is all too easy to be distracted by process stories, and talking points. But elections are more significant than that. They decide the course of a country's future. As this campaign intensifies it is becoming clearer by the day that the next general election will be more than a jostle between party tactics. Instead, it will be a clash of ideals and beliefs, values and principles.

I know it has sometimes been fashionable over recent years to say there are no big differences any more between the major political parties. But, as this campaign is now showing, there are. And it goes beyond merely what the parties try to highlight or what they campaign on, important though these are in exemplifying what the parties believe. It goes to the heart of the policies — and the very values — they stand for.

On the one side stand Labour values of justice, fairness and opportunity symbolised in our determination to campaign on the economy and the public services and our policy commitments to increase investment in those services, to lift pensioners and children out of poverty, to help

families balance work and home, to bring the prospect of home ownership within reach for many more young families.

Britain has always worked well for those who are privileged. Our
mission is for Britain to work for the many not the few. Our election
manifesto will build on the agenda that we have set out in our five-year
plans and Gordon Brown's recent Budget. I believe it will be a more
detailed, more radical, more ambitious prospectus for the progressive
modernisation of Britain than the manifestos we presented to the public
either in 1997 or in 2001.

On the other side stand Conservative values symbolised by the
current turmoil inside the Tory Party. Mr Howard Flight has opened a
veritable Pandora's box. He has thrown a spotlight on policies and principles that infuse today's Conservative Party. When last week Mr Flight
called for public spending to be reduced by more than the £35 billion the
Conservatives already plan, his was not a lone voice. He is speaking for
a Conservative obsession that is shared by Mr Redwood, Lord Saatchi,
even Mr Letwin and Mr Howard—to radically reduce the size of the
state and its share of national income not to 40 per cent but to 35 per
cent. I believe their view of the world is wrong but it is perfectly legitimate to hold it. What is not legitimate is to hide it.

Mr Flight has exposed the truth about today's Conservatives: they
have a Thatcherite ideological obsession that is deep and real. Where—
as they put it themselves—people are big and the state is small. Where
individuals make their own way. Where privilege gets its own reward.
It is this view of the world that took them to oppose our plans for investment in health and education, our plans to extend parental leave, our
plans to make a university education accessible to half of our young
people. It is why the Conservatives do not support our target—still less
our ambition—to first halve and then eliminate child poverty.

It is not opposition to poverty. It is support for privilege. That is where
today's Conservative Party stands. So it is not just what it did in office
that haunts the Tories. Both the nature of its current campaign and its
proposals for the future show that the Conservative Party is resorting to

type. It is opportunist. It is hard right. It is keen to exploit problems but its cupboard is bare when it comes to dealing with them. Above all, the Tories are unchanged and unreformed. Their belief is not that they lost because the Thatcherite revolution went too far but that it did not go far enough. They have a new leader but they are an old party. And they are clinging to old certainties from the past. As Mr Howard himself puts it, 'our principles haven't changed, our values haven't changed'.

Its flagship public service policy — paying subsidies from the taxpayer for patients and parents to go private, thereby depriving state schools and NHS hospitals of investment — is a symptom of a Conservative Party that remains obsessed with privilege for a few, when it ought be fixated with opening up opportunities for all.

In an election campaign, dividing lines of this sort matter. They matter in this campaign more than most. After eight years in government, the obvious danger is that the campaign turns into a referendum on the Labour Party and not a choice between parties. So it is important to draw out the real contrast between where we stand and where our opponents stand. Elections are, after all, a choice between competing futures. For that reason, it is even more important to set out with clarity and conviction our positive agenda and purpose for a third term.

For me, it is simple and it is clear. It is to do what it says on every Labour Party membership card: to put wealth, power and opportunity in the hands of the many, not the few. To build an opportunity society where the chance to get on is extended from a privileged few to all who are prepared to work hard and play by the rules, so that Britain becomes a nation based on merit, not class.

In these last eight years, we have laid the foundations on which to build such an ambition. Britain is moving forwards. And it's easy to forget how far we have come. The country Labour inherited in 1997 was one where decades of economic instability had taken its toll. Today, a strong and stable economy is the rock on which a Labour third term will be built. With Labour, Britain has witnessed the longest period of economic growth since records began, an economy now bigger than that of Italy and France. Interest rates and mortgage rates lower than at any point since the 1960s – half the rate they were under the Tories.

In 1997, social exclusion, division and poverty were accepted as facts of life in Britain. Millions were denied a living wage. One in three children grew up in poverty, and one in five families had no one in work. Today we have the lowest unemployment and highest employment rate of any of our competitors for the first time since the 1950s. Living standards are up for everyone – and for the poorest up most – thanks to the minimum wage and policies specifically helping working families with children. We are bringing about the biggest decreases in child and pensioner poverty the country has ever seen.

In 1997 under-investment meant that the public goods most European countries took for granted – high quality universal childcare provision, modern public buildings, schools and hospitals with modern equipment and well-paid staff – were largely absent in Britain. Today our public services are being revitalised. Britain is experiencing the biggest increases in public service investment the country has ever seen. In the NHS waiting times are down. In state schools, results are up. The number of state-educated entrants to our top universities has risen by more than a third since 1997 without compromising high standards, a potent symbol of upward mobility.

And there is more. Then, Britain's constitution was grid-locked. Today, a modern pluralist democracy is developing: devolution for Scotland and Wales, House of Lords reform, freedom of information and the Human Rights Act. Our inner cities – long abandoned – are being regenerated. Childcare, at the bottom of the political priority list then, is now at the top.

The sum of these changes is even more important than their parts. There is, I believe, a renewed pride in Britain, a real sense of progress symbolised by the public belief that the British economy is moving in the right direction. In the 1980s, the consensus was that Britain must inevitably fall behind. Today, a new consensus is emerging that Britain can move ahead. Then it was nostalgia about the past. Now it is hope about the future. The fatalism of the old consensus is giving way to the optimism of the new.

So, in eight years we have made good progress. But it is nowhere near enough. It is true that steadily things are getting better for people. But life remains tough for many. Injustice has been tackled but it has not yet been overcome, whether it is the scar of Africa abroad or the indignity of poverty at home.

So we cannot rest on what we have done. Instead we must use it as a springboard for even faster progress. After eight years in office, this is not the time to rest on our laurels, but to renew the New Labour project for a third term. We have to win the battle not just of votes—but the battle of ideas. That way the centre-left sets the agenda and the political landscape is forged in the image of our values, not those of the right.

We need to quicken the pace of change principally because we are hungry to realise our values of fairness and social justice. But beneath this moral imperative lies a practical one. Our insight today is that Britain can only succeed economically if we are mobile socially. Britain's success in a globally competitive economy depends on unlocking the talents of all our people. Every talent wasted is not just a loss to the individual, but a drag on the country. A knowledge economy needs an opportunity society. There is a glass ceiling on opportunity in our country. After eight years in government, we have raised it—but in truth, we have not yet broken it.

We cannot do that by returning to the past. Britain has to move beyond old notions of class hierarchy and privilege if we are to succeed in the future. This is why the Conservatives have got it so wrong. Their support for an education system that provides excellence for a privileged few will not work in an era when the modern economy calls for good schooling and high skills to be available to all. The Conservatives cannot meet the challenges of the future because they are continually looking to the past.

To succeed, Britain has to modernise. And by that I don't mean simply becoming a high-tech, high-skill economy. I mean becoming an open, mobile classless society. It is progressive modernisation that Britain needs in order to compete and win in today's world.

The Labour Party was founded on a belief that it is the duty of government not just to attack entrenched privileges that hold people back, but to promote equality of life-chances across the economy, politics and culture. As the socialist writer GDH Cole argued in 1943: 'It ought to be so obvious as hardly to need stating that it is an obligation falling upon any decent human society to give all its members a fair chance in life'.

Six decades later we still crave a Britain in which people can go as far as they have the talent to go, where prosperity and opportunity are widely shared. Doing so has to mean getting social mobility moving again in Britain. I believe that must be at the core of our ambitions for a Labour third term. It should form the basis of our progressive modernising policies.

First, an economic policy that places renewed emphasis on high skills, not low wages as the best route to full employment in every region and nation of Britain. Economic stability is fundamental, but it is investment in knowledge and technology that holds the key to Britain's future competitiveness. That is why in any third term we need to place as much emphasis on vocational education and skills training as in our first two terms we put on academic education and school standards. A world of ever faster change makes lifelong learning a necessity, not a luxury.

The budget has committed an additional £65 million to Employer Training Pilots, and an extra £1.5 billion to the renewal and renovation of Further Education colleges. There will be Education Maintenance Allowances of up to £75 a week to ensure 90 per cent of 17 year olds stay on in recognised training or education by 2007. And there will be a new commitment — to ensure all school leavers have the choice of a place in training, in sixth-form, or in a Modern Apprenticeship.

Second, a welfare strategy that puts a premium on independence, not dependence, lifting people out of poverty and making work pay through a rising minimum wage. Employability is the route map both to greater economic success and faster social mobility. Our employment record is excellent, but we should not rest until everyone who wants a job has a job. We know that one million incapacity benefit claimants say that they want to work, if only they were given the right level of support. There will be new rules to encourage IB claimants into work, and further reforms to housing benefit, with an extension of the £2,000 work bonus for single parents. So a renewed drive on welfare reform should be the partner of our drive to rid Britain of child and pensioner poverty.

Third, an education policy that makes excellence available to all, not just some. As the premium on knowledge in the modern economy becomes ever greater, education becomes more, not less significant as the true motor of economic and social mobility. Educational excellence for an elite will no longer do for a modern Britain in a more competitive world.

Hence the need to create a new universal system of childcare provision so that every child gets the best start in life. Research tells us that for every £1 invested in early years, £7 is saved in lower crime, better jobs, and higher educational outcomes in later life. There will be 1000 Sure Start centres throughout the country. Free early years education of 15 hours a week will be available for every three and four year old, with an extra one million childcare places. And so too the need to invest and reform our system of primary and secondary education to make high standards and fair choice available not just to some parents and pupils but to all.

Fourth, a public services policy that makes personalised education and healthcare available to those without wealth, and not just those with it. Our programme for further investment and change will keep public service values intact but their systems will be reformed. So that tax-based universal services are capable of meeting modern and diverse needs. Today, people who can afford it buy choice over health and education. Those without do without. This is unfair, and should be changed. A modern progressive approach calls for choice to be redistributed, not ignored. So with capacity being built and with services improving both parents and patients will be able to have a greater say and more choice, not by having to pay but as of right. That will help drive hospital waiting times down to their lowest level ever: a maximum wait of just 18 weeks.

Fifth, an assets policy that empowers families to progress. Giving more people an economic stake in society can not only help tackle poverty but unlock aspiration and foster independence. So at one end of the age spectrum we will develop the Child Trust Fund 'baby bond' to give every youngster a nest egg for the future. If Labour wins a third term, payments to the Child Trust Fund will be extended not just to the primary years, but to the secondary years too, building savings and wealth for every child. At the other end we will pilot new approaches so that pensioners have individual budgets to control how they are cared for in old age. And as we invest in housing, we will help more first time buyers own their own homes and help more tenants take an equity stake in their homes.

Sixth, a governance policy that empowers local communities to have a greater say. Globalisation is driving people to take refuge in what they know – their families and communities. If politics and services are to command trust and legitimacy, they need to be structured to reflect that yearning. Reforms to re-invigorate local government and pass power downwards and outwards to local communities give people the chance to exercise greater control in their lives, for example in combating street level disorder and enhancing community liveability. The plans are about finding new ways of allying the authorities – whether they are police or councils – with the majority in every community who work hard and play by the rules, against the minority who do not.

These policies are about translating traditional Labour values into the modern world. They are new means to old ends. And just as the governments of Clement Attlee and Margaret Thatcher fundamentally changed the political landscape so they provide the basis for Tony

Blair's government to do the same. These policies can entrench a lasting New Labour settlement in Britain.

Over the next decade we can move power irreversibly to those who use public services and the communities that rely on them. Doing things to people will no longer do. In today's world it is doing things with them that holds the key, whether to improving health, fighting crime or improving neighbourhoods. Modern progressive government should seek to rebalance rights and responsibilities in a new contract between state and citizen, where government provides opportunities and citizens strive to take them. This is the means to reward work and effort and ambition and enterprise. It is the means to take for New Labour the banner of aspiration and ambition. And it is the means to reconnect with those who form the backbone of Britain—working people, middle and low income alike, hard-working families—who want to know there are fair rules in play, and there is a government on their side working hard to put those rules in place.

And it is here we have such a fundamental difference of principle with the Conservatives. For them, government's role must be reduced, not reformed. Unlike the Conservatives we are not prepared to see citizens sink or swim in a sea of change. Indeed, as change becomes ever faster—sometimes bewilderingly so—we believe people need government on their side.

There is a big divide in British politics between those who believe that more people can make the grade, who are optimistic that more people can get on, and are determined to help them do so, and those who want to bang shut the doors of opportunity in our country, to hang up a sign saying 'no vacancies', who run down our country's success, who are profoundly pessimistic about the potential of ordinary people to get on. That is why the Conservatives are determined to abandon school targets, cap university places, cut Sure Start, and enable people to opt out of public services rather than helping the majority to access better services available to all on the basis of need, not ability to pay.

One way points to the past and privilege—the other, the future and opportunity. Our message is simple: if you fear a return to the past vote against it; if you value progress vote for it. We have a once in a lifetime chance at this next election. To see off the last hurrah of Thatcherism. To entrench progressive change.

The mandate we seek is to go further and faster in breaking down the barriers that hold too many people back. Our goal: social justice. A fair society, where no-one is left behind, where all can bridge the gap between what they are and what they have it in themselves to become. A country that is open to the innate talents of people according to their worth, not birth.

That is the Britain we seek. We ask you to help us make it happen.

Response by Lisa Harker

The 2005 general election may come to be remembered for being a referendum on Tony Blair's leadership, the Tory comeback that didn't happen, or a new beginning for three-party politics. But one thing is certain: it won't be remembered as a battle of ideas about the kind of society that each of the main political parties would hope to build.

Why is this? Alan Milburn's speech reminds us that the desire for ideological debate is not extinguished, but neither is it burning bright. Over the past decade, politics in general has been 'ideology-lite'. New Labour in particular has lacked a guiding philosophy. Indeed, it has sought to make a virtue of the fact that it has moved beyond traditional ideologies of Left and Right and has instead been driven by 'what works'. And by neither setting out its values nor its overarching beliefs, Labour has found it increasingly difficult to have a conversation with the electorate about the society it hopes to build.

Even at its boldest, Labour has struggled with championing its vision of a better future, preferring to achieve greater social justice by stealth. Its most impressive aspiration—the pledge to eradicate child poverty in a generation—remains, as the Fabian Society's Life Chances and Child Poverty Commission research has shown, one of the government's best kept secrets.

84

Alan Milburn

Some of the reticence about setting out a vision of a more progressive future stems from a fear about electoral credibility. The spectre of the 1992 election defeat still hangs over the Party. Bold pledges, such as eradicating child poverty or creating a universal childcare system that is affordable for all, imply a level of redistribution of resources that our current tax system simply does not allow. The 'tax problem' means that politicians avoid turning the spotlight on their long-term ambitions, preferring instead to talk about the short-term targets that can be met within current spending plans. As a result the electorate is left feeling disorientated about the future.

Three further obstacles stand in the way of politicians making a clear case for a more progressive future. Firstly, the language often used tends to be alienating. Talk of improving 'social mobility' or 'building a progressive consensus' does not resonate far beyond academia. A more open and inclusive language needs to be found to describe the kind of society that we wish to build, if hearts and minds beyond the Westminster village are to be won over.

Secondly, the statistics that are often used to describe the society in which we live fail to stir interest or emotions. Are we surprised that there seems to be little appetite for a drive to eradicate child poverty when we describe the problem in terms of the number of children living below 60 per cent of the median income? Statistics do matter, but we have perhaps over-relied on them to make a case for change. The Fabian Society's Commission on Life Chances and Child Poverty has demonstrated that public attitudes towards poverty soften when described in terms of real life experience rather than expressed in numbers.

Finally, the corrosive relationship between politicians and the media undermines attempts at ideological debate. It is almost impossible for a politician to set out a utopian vision of the future without being either pilloried or ignored. This mess is not entirely of the media's making, of course; politicians obsessed with media management and adversarial debate are also culpable. Whatever the reason, there is little doubting the difficulty that politicians now find themselves in. Despite living in an age of media mass communication, they are struggling to have a meaningful conversation about the future with the electorate.

So it appears not to be a lack of ideas that has prevented Labour from championing a vision of the 'good society' but a number of other obstacles: the absence of a governing philosophy, the lack of suitable expression for its ideas and the difficulty in finding a means of conveying its message. No doubt these obstacles are linked and have reinforced one another. But nor are they insurmountable.

Within Labour's manifesto lie some impressive policy commitments. To my mind, the most impressive relate to children's life chances: the commitment to end child poverty once and for all, to develop of a new pillar of the welfare state in the form of asset-based welfare and to build a universal, high quality childcare system which is affordable to all. Each one of these policies has an in-built sense of destination, and together they make up part of a picture of a better society.

Labour's friends have urged the Party to engage its heart, spell out its values and set out the kind of society that it wants for Britain. The third term offers perhaps the last opportunity to do just that.

Lisa Harker is Chair of the Daycare Trust

8 | Ruth Kelly
'The comprehensive ideal'

It is a pleasure to talk to a Fabian audience. I know how central the Society's work has been in recent years and how central it will continue to be. Not least in the areas of poverty and life chances. This is what we are talking about today. I want to argue that views on life chances, on social mobility, represent a central dividing line in British politics. Does Britain want a Tory government which hardly even pays lip-service to this agenda? Or does it want a Labour government which works tirelessly to make it reality?

I then want to relate the debate to education policy. Yesterday's education system is not necessarily suited to today's world. We must keep focused on our aims. I will outline why I think it is that this demands moving beyond just having comprehensive schools to having a genuinely comprehensive education system.

The demands of greater equality of opportunity

So why do the politics of 'life chances' represent such a key dividing line in modern politics? A strong sense of social justice has always been at the heart of centre left politics. And an attachment to improved 'life-chances' or 'equality of opportunity' is one element of this. But what does this really mean? What do we, as progressive politicians, really care about?

Well, I believe that ultimately what matters is giving every individual the chance to flourish—the chance to achieve their potential. There is nothing more depressing than people being pessimistic about the future — be it in their own or in their children's lives — simply because of the place in life that they find themselves born into. Instilling a sense of expectation and aspiration in people is at the heart of my politics.

When we focus on 'life chances' we tap into people's deeply held emotions. Everyone wants their children to succeed. And everyone wants the opportunity to make their life better. This is certainly the case when I meet and talk to people on the doorstep in Bolton.

This is why the 1980s were so soul destroying. So many children's lives wasted. And so many adults who couldn't look forward to the next year with hope. But it was more than soul destroying. It was bad for Britain. To paraphrase John Smith, it was a criminal waste of the extraordinary talents of ordinary British people.

Now that is why the upcoming election is so important. We must make it clear that only Labour recognises how demanding the expansion of life-chances can be. It is only Labour which recognises that government has a duty to ensure more than just equality before the law, the formal right to vote or freedom from discrimination — important though these rights are.

Labour also recognises that social justice has at its heart a deeper and more demanding sense of fairness. A fairness which demands that an individual's outcomes in life should not be primarily determined by their background — by their social class, their parent's income, their gender or their ethnicity.

Only Labour understands the implications of this for politics. The right flirts with the language of equality of opportunity. John Major talked of a 'classless society'. Michael Howard recently stated that one of his key beliefs was that 'people must have every opportunity to fulfil their potential.' They know this is what people want to hear. But fundamentally I do not think they understand what this means in practice. They do not understand the demands of creating more equal life chances.

So this, for me, is a key dividing line in modern politics. While the centre-left understands the importance of politics and government action in fashioning more equal life chances—the right just does not. And if you do not will the means, you are not serious about the ends.

While the centre-left understands the damage that subsidising the education of a privileged few will do—the Tories do not. Why else would they back voucher schemes that would take £1 billion straight out of state schools budgets to subsidise the education of the few? Why else would they want to bring back selection? Something we will not do. Why else would they threaten investment in education with pledges to reduce spending?

We on the centre-left have a vision where politics and collective decision making is central. A vision where government plays a role in laying the foundations for greater equality of opportunity. Of course there are limits to what government can and should do; individuals have the prime responsibilities here. But there are vital roles for government to help people to 'get on' and to achieve their potential. Markets in the main are forces for good. But they have their limits. People must not just be left to the mercy of market forces but supported and equipped to achieve in a market economy.

It is a vision which has gained strength from much that has been achieved in recent years:

- We have pledged to abolish child poverty and have made a good start.
- We have made unprecedented investment in early years services—with more to come.
- We have opened up new debates about the importance of assets—the first Child Trust Fund accounts will be opened in the next few days.
- And for adults, we have achieved record levels of employment, improved rights at work, and have made the transformation of skills a priority

But what about education policy? Again good progress has been made. By 2007/8 school funding will be twice the level it was in 1997. There are now more teachers in schools than at any point in the last 20 years — 28,000 more than in 1997 and 105,000 new support staff. The hard work of these professionals has resulted in improved standards. Our focus on the basics has led to what Ofsted has described as a 'transformation' of literacy standards in prmary schools. Flagship initiaitves such as 'Excellence in Cities' and 'London Challenge' have resulted in the biggest gains being achieved for the most disadvantaged. I am immensely proud of these achievements. They make a difference to the lives of people who matter to us.

And we must continue our relentless approach to driving up standards for all children. Never accepting that what is good enough for children from better off backgrounds is too good for those from poorer ones.

At times this will mean tough decisions — closing schools that underperform, bringing in new schools including Academies in areas of need, allowing schools that are popular with parents to expand, trying to give all parents the reality of more choice among good local schools so this is not just something for those who can opt out of the system. Tough decsions, but ones taken with clear aims of social mobility and life chances at their core.

We have also made progress on other key issues We have adopted a zero tolerance approach to poor discipline. Teachers and other pupils should not tolerate even day-to-day disruption in the classroom, let alone more severe incidents. Heads with the tools they need. And parents taking their responsibilities seriously.

I welcome all ideas on how we can improve behaviour, and I'm glad that there is increasingly a shared view between government, unions and the wider profession on this issue. We have built a strong relationship with teachers. More funding and stability for schools. Higher pay. Lighter touch Ofsted inspections coming in. In the future I want to see teacher appraisal become more focused on teaching and learning. And better support for professional development.

Of course, we will have our differences from time to time on specific issues, but no one should underestimate the commitment of a Labour government to those working in public services and in our schools and colleges in particular. Without them our aspirations for our nation would come to nought.

We need to build on these solid foundations. But how? Put simply — I want our education system to complete a shift from one where 'comprehensive schools' have been the almost exclusive focus, to one where we provide a 'genuine comprehensive education'. I want to work with teachers and parents to achieve this. And I want further improvements in standards across the board but most of all for the most disadvantaged.

There is a feeling sometimes that the word 'comprehensive' can get in the way of productive debate. I think that is regrettable. The comprehensive ideal was and remains powerful and inspiring. It reflects our fundamental view that all children are of equal worth. The challenge is to reinterpret this ideal in the light of the challenges of today.

The belief which drove politicians like Tony Crosland, who forced through reform, is the same belief that should drive us now. It is a passionate conviction that all children, from whatever background, are alike in their capacity to reason, to imagine, to aspire to a successful and rewarding life and to achieve their full potential.

In the 1960s this meant rejecting the flawed science and blatant injustice of the eleven-plus. And it also demanded structural change to a system in which children's futures were, in large part, decided on their performance on one day when they were eleven with virtually no chance of movement after this. Comprehensive schools played a vital role in overcoming the inherent injustices of the post war system. For some they were the springboard to opportunity.

Overall standards have improved in the past 30 years. And one thing I am particularly struck by is the picture for girls. In 1973 just 73,000 girls achieved five good GCSEs or more — last year the figure was 186,000. But the comprehensive schools created in the 1960s and 1970s had limitations:

• First, the focus was almost entirely on children of secondary school age, and mostly on ending the eleven plus.

• Second, there was little agreement on what it meant to provide a high quality education once children were inside the school gate. As long as people were not selected this was good enough for some.

• Third, schools also tended to take on a single model, with little scope for innovative leadership or the ability to develop a distinctive character or ethos.

• Fourth, too often poverty became an excuse for poor performance. In too many areas comprehensive schools divided into 'good' middle class and 'bad' working class schools with children in the latter not getting the education they deserved.

• And fifth, users — parents and pupils — were not placed at the heart of reform. Crosland's famous circular 10/65 — requesting that local authorities embrace comprehensive principles — did not even mention consulting parents on such significant changes.

These are strong drawbacks. The 1960s and 1970s were very different from the diverse, less deferential world in which we live today. Aspiring to provide a uniform service — successful or otherwise — cannot be the basis for a modern comprehensive system.

Reform was — and still is — essential because the traditional model of comprehensive schooling did not transform educational opportunities in the way that many hoped it would.

Just as Crosland wanted reform because he was motivated by changing children's outcomes — a deep sense of what he called social equality — we should also hold our policies up to the harsh glare of a social justice test.

Many of you here today will know that the facts on social mobility make for depressing reading. As the middle classes expanded after the war there was considerable movement. But since the early 1960s social mobility has declined. Studies which compare a group born in 1958 with a group born in 1970 show that the later group has experienced lower levels of social mobility. That means that for people in their thirties the social class of their parents matters more than it did in the past.

Though the reasons behind this are complex, it is clear that comprehensive schools have not been the engine of social mobility and equality that Crosland wanted them to be. They played a vital role in overcoming the institutionalised two-tierism that was inherent in selection, but for too many people they did not deliver the transformation of life chances.

The challenge we now face is how to revitalise and make a reality of the comprehensive ideal given concrete expression by Crosland. The challenge, I think, is moving from thinking merely about comprehensive schools to thinking about a vision of a genuinely comprehensive education system. Achieving this will involve at least three strands. They are:

• Creating a comprehensive and tailored education system within schools.
• Achieving a genuinely comprehensive local education system
• And developing a system which educates children from 3 to 19.

Comprehensive education within schools

Let me take fashioning comprehensive education within schools first. Differences between schools shape children's outcomes in important ways. But different experiences within schools are also vital. Just because you go to a good school does not guarantee success.

This is why many schools started tailoring learning long before 'personalisation' became a buzz word. Building on this experience, my vision is of such a tailored learning experience for all individual children. One which recognises where children excel and where they can be given extra help to nurture their talents. And one which recognizes where children are falling behind—particularly in core skills like reading and writing.

This tailoring can occur within a whole classroom setting. But I want government to support schools and the teaching profession to develop further the role of small group tuition as well.

I see this as a real extension of choice, of putting the users of the education system — pupils and their parents — firmly in the driving seat. Of course parents want a say in choosing which school their child attends — and we must strive to make this work better. But that is just one discrete — albeit important — decision.

Parents want more than that. They want to be updated and informed about their child's progress on a regular basis. They want to be involved in the numerous decisions about their child's learning. They want to have a say about the wider activities that their child can benefit from beyond the school day and beyond the school gate.

When parents are engaged and informed like this children and teachers alike benefit. We know that levels of parental interest in a child's learning shape outcomes. And we know that parents from disadvantaged backgrounds sometimes feel less able to play this supportive role.

If we get this right there is a promise of a virtuous circle. Parents, working with teachers, driving for a more tailored learning in schools. And parents taking their responsibilities seriously — more involved in their child learning at home and more likely to ensure their child attends school ready to learn.

Parents will also play a central role in improving the quality of school meals. Government is providing increased funding and getting the framework right. But we are also supporting parents in this area to drive change. The new School Food Trust will give parents information and advice to work with schools to meet tough new standards. It all adds up to a massive opportunity. Building on Jamie Oliver's inspirational work we have the chance to achieve the step-change in the quality of school food.

Comprehensive education systems

The second element of change is fashioning a truly comprehensive education system. Because the needs and aspirations of individual pupils are so varied and demand such flexibility, it is unlikely that any single institution will be able to fulfil them satisfactorily, however hard

94

it tries. For this reason the whole system—not only individual schools—must be geared around the needs of individual pupils.

As more schools become specialist schools, as we encourage greater innovation, diversity and experimentation, the system as a whole will become more varied. A wealth of expertise will be there to draw on. One great challenge in the coming decade will be ensuring that this enrichment benefits all pupils.

We have already moved policy on from one dictated by a culture of dependence on central government, to one of strong, autonomous institutions. Now we need to take the next step. We need to work towards a culture which recognises the added value of carefully developed interdependence.

I see the 14-19 reforms as an example of this. Engaging learners at this time and tailoring provision and options to the needs and preferences of the individual student. That demands that schools and other providers offer greater choice and flexibility to young people.

It is unlikely that any one institution alone will be able to provide the full range of opportunities that the 14-19 reforms require. So instead the 14-19 learning environment will increasingly become one where young people can learn in more than one institution.

A 14-year-old may for instance spend four days a week in their school on the core National Curriculum and spend the other beginning a specialised diploma at a FE College. A 17 year old may spend two days in a school sixth form and the rest of the week in work experience or on a high quality level three engineering diploma.

A sixth-form student wanting to learn Mandarin may spend some time at a different school specialising in languages. Clearly such a system demands schools, colleges, employers, the local authority and the local LSC to work closely together. With schools, I have already outlined how I expect every secondary school to be part of a group working together to manage behaviour provision by September 2007.

This is one example of how schools, supported by local authorities, can achieve outcomes better together and ensure they all have access to the widest possible range of support. Not collaboration for its own sake, but collaboration with a clear purpose.

But there will be other ways in which a truly comprehensive education system would see schools working together with each other, and with a wealth of other providers, to match different expertise to the needs of pupils.

Comprehensive education: 3-19

For the third element of change, let me turn to creating a 'comprehensive education system from': 3 to19. Education is not just about schools. Children learn from the moment they are born. We are discovering more and more about the importance of the early years in shaping later life outcomes. Study after study continues to confirm that the significant investment that this government is making in Sure Start, children's centres and enhancing the choices for parents of young children, is right. That is why it is so important that we have made early years a core part of the modern welfare state.

And education and learning cannot just be allowed to stop when children turn sixteen. We want to make the old school leaving age a thing of the past. We have set the ambitious target of moving, over a decade from 75 per cent of 17 year olds in learning to 90 per cent. That will require the best specialist and vocational education we have ever seen in this country. The overall parameters are clear — not a learning experience of 5-16 but one from three to 19. In the next five years better integration of the different phases of education will become important. Helping parents and children manage transitions into primary school, into secondary and then into post 14 learning, will become more important.

So these are what I see as the three elements of a genuinely comprehensive education system:

One: Comprehensive education within schools
Two: A comprehensive local education system
Three: learning from the early years through to 19

Working with parents and teachers. All driving towards higher standards but also higher levels of equity. If we get this right then the prize is enormous.

Building on solid foundations laid in the first two terms, a third term could embed progressive change. It could secure for Labour a legacy of the best educated generation of children ever.

By drawing on the best of comprehensive schools but making the system work for all we have a real opportunity in a third term to fundamentally change life chances and to be a historic force for social justice.

Response by Geoff Whitty

Ruth Kelly's determination that no individual's life chances should be unfairly determined by their background is very welcome, as is her recognition of the particular significance of social class. Much more emphasis needs to be placed within education policy on combating the continuing importance of class as a determinant of educational outcomes. Comparative evidence suggests that its influence is especially strong in Britain when compared with other European countries, and particularly with the Nordic countries that have strong social democratic traditions. So, while increasing attention has rightly been given to gender and 'race' by Labour policy makers in recent years, the continuing—and much greater—impact of social class must not be ignored.

Ruth's recognition of this builds on that part of Labour's recent Five Year Strategy for Children and Learners which highlighted the huge influence of social class in this country. It was illustrated with a telling graph which showed children from lower social class homes with high early test scores being overtaken—even while in primary school—by higher social class children who had started with low test scores.

New Labour's early years policies have, of course, long been informed by such findings, as evidenced in the various interventions that make up Sure Start and recent approaches to integrated children's services. Indeed, Ruth's first major speech as Secretary of State drew on research based here at the Institute to show that high quality pre-school experiences can have lasting effects. Current policies

97

in this field may therefore offer real hope for the future.

While making early years provision a core part of the modern welfare state for tackling social class disadvantage, we must beware of neglecting the needs of those currently in school. We need to identify what will help—or certainly not make matters worse for—those who have already suffered from inequalities in the early years. Ruth's emphasis on the importance of coherent and comprehensive provision from three through to 19 is therefore welcome.

Yet I still worry about some of the policies advocated for schools, especially in later sections of the Five Year Strategy. My own research and my understanding of other evidence suggests that some of them could actually exacerbate rather than mitigate the effects of social class on educational attainment and participation—unless they are handled very carefully indeed.

Here I will give just two examples—one concerns secondary provision; the other the response to Tomlinson. I recognise that policies are made for all sorts of reasons, not all to do with the findings of educational research. But, whatever the rights and wrongs of these policies, it is important that they are now implemented in ways that will help to close the attainment gap rather than widen it.

I welcome Ruth's emphasis on a comprehensive system of education and on tailored education within schools. But, at the same time as fostering diversity in comprehensive secondary education, we do need to ensure an academic and social mix in our schools if we are to maximise achievement—particularly among the disadvantaged. There are still too many urban schools which have been colonised by particular social groups, either deliberately or by default.

The more schools in an area that are their own admissions authorities, the greater the extent of academic and social polarisation. The benefits of increased school autonomy need therefore to be tempered by a recognition of this danger. Full implementation of last year's recommendations on school admissions from the Select Committee would help here. The new emphasis on collaboration could also help, but we need greater incentives to encourage it. Current accountability measures almost all work in the opposite direction.

With regard to 14-19 qualifications, the government's alternative to the Tomlinson proposals may not be the best way of enhancing the status and quality of vocational education. Given the evidence on social class bias—and indeed gender and race bias—in the selection of different options and the life-time consequences of this, we need to ensure that the new programmes are designed in ways that limit these effects. This would have been an issue even under the full Tomlinson framework, but we will need to take even greater care in its absence.

If we are to enhance the relative life chances of the disadvantaged, we need to give at least as much attention to the inclusion agenda as the standards agenda. We must also seek a proper balance between institutional independence and interdependence in the quest for social justice. But, of course, we need anyway to be realistic about the impact of education policy on social inequalities. Education policies alone are never likely to eradicate social inequalities in education, so we now need joined up economic and social policies that go well beyond the early years.

Geoff Whitty is Director of the Institute of Education

9 | Yvette Cooper
'We have not yet gone far enough'

I would like to thank the Fabian Society for organizing this series of lectures on life chances, and also for the work of their Commission on Child Poverty and Life Chances. For the Fabian Society concern with child poverty, inequality and injustice has always been at the heart of their work. Indeed the very first Fabian Society tract, published after the Match Girls strike in 1888, was called *Why Are The Many Poor?* Championing the cause of the many not the few has always been the rationale for the Fabian Society, just as it has been the political purpose of the Labour Party through its history too.

But this series of lectures and the work of the Commission on Life Chances and Child Poverty are, I believe, particularly significant. As the interim report of the Fabian Society Commission on Life Chances and Child Poverty makes clear, their ambition is to 'reshape the wider political and public debates about poverty and inequality in Britain'; to build 'a new settlement, a new political consensus, if the decision not to accept poverty in our society is to prove as politically robust as Clement Attlee's National Health Service became after 1951.'

These are bold aims. But they are also essential aims. They are critical to our purpose in the Labour Party, and in the Labour government, and also to our future as a nation.

This is the fifth of the Fabian series of lectures on life chances. Already David Miliband has set out why improving life chances is a vital part of a modern social democratic approach, and why Labour today is well placed to entrench those values at the heart of a modern political settlement. John Reid has argued strongly for the importance of empowering people and raising aspirations, particularly for improving health. Ruth Kelly set out a passionate case for developing every child's talents, and the further improvements she is championing for our schools. And Alan Milburn has set out Labour's purpose to smash the glass ceiling on opportunities, and the clear dividing lines this leaves with the Conservatives.

In the final lecture in the series I want to return to the point where the Fabian Society started, to child poverty, life chances and the need for a political consensus. I want to explain why I think the crusade to widen life chances for all is so important for Labour's third term election campaign, for our moral and political purpose as a party, and for the future of our nation.

I believe that the aims of cutting child poverty and widening life chances for all should command wide and strong support across society. After all, this is a progressive programme, which benefits not simply those suffering greatest disadvantage, but everyone whose potential is still denied.

The challenges we face ahead as an economy and as a society mean that the Conservative approach to these issues would be deeply destructive and divisive, and would be to the detriment not just of the most vulnerable, but to our economic prosperity and the cohesion of society as a whole.

Just as John Reid has talked about health care, and Ruth Kelly has talked about education, I want also to say something specifically about how housing and sustainable communities impact on life chances too. And finally I want to support David's conclusions about how we—and the Fabian Society—need to do more to build the progressive consensus so that no one dare turn the clock back on poverty again.

Child Poverty Matters

The left has always felt passionately about the alleviation of poverty. The Labour Party over the decades has championed support for those who are vulnerable and excluded. But for all the progress in the middle of the twentieth century, the final decades saw a shocking rise in child poverty, fuelled by Conservative policies at the time. The trebling of child poverty between 1979 and 1997 (and the prevalent view that this was somehow the unavoidable and even acceptable price of rising prosperity) was a scar on British society.

After all, no one had any doubt about the impact of poverty on a child's life. We are not just talking about the short term distress of a nine year old unable to afford to go on a school trip, or the resentment of a 12 year old because their family can't go on holiday again. Poverty in childhood haunts people for the rest of their lives. Children growing up in poverty get worse results at school, are more likely to become teenage parents, more likely to be unemployed, and are more likely to be parents in poverty themselves twenty years later. They just don't get a fair chance in life.

That is why the Labour government's ambition to end child poverty in a generation is so important—and so revolutionary. It is hard to underestimate what a fundamental shift this is in approach compared to the Conservative years. It is a moral cause for all those who care about injustice and unfairness. But it is also, as the Fabian Commission has pointed out, in the interests of our economy and our society as a whole that generations of children should not see their talents wasted and their potential denied.

The progress we have made so far has surprised many. One million children have been lifted out of poverty. According to LSE academic John Hills, 'The package of support for low income working families with children is one of the most generous in the world.'

Of course there will be challenges ahead in sustaining that progress. We know too that it isn't just about income, it's about the opportunity for parents to learn and earn, and the chance for babies and children to get support from programmes like Sure Start in the very early years of life. Labour is addressing not just poverty but social exclusion too. So rough sleeping is down by two thirds, families are no longer kept in bed and breakfast accommodation, and support has increased for those most marginalized from society.

And the evidence shows that the extra investment is making a difference where it counts. Jane Waldfogel's research has shown that when parents on low income were given extra cash they didn't spend it on fags and booze as the stereotype suggests. Quite the reverse. They spent the extra money on the kids.

But where have the Conservatives been in the debate on child poverty? We know their record. Child poverty trebled. And this was not simply the result of indifference, or the failure to respond to a wider economic problem. The Conservative government actually cut child benefit in real terms. They even changed the law to remove the duty on the government to consider an increase in child benefit. By 1997 child benefit was still lower in real terms than it had been in 1979. Frankly it is astonishing to believe they could have got away with cutting support for children across the board. It just shows how far we have come — and also perhaps how much we already take for granted in the way the political climate has changed.

Even today, when the Conservative party professes a concern for public services, they still have nothing to say about child poverty. We have heard nothing in response to our target to abolish child poverty. Over the past few years they have repeatedly said they would cut Sure Start, and they opposed the introduction of tax credits. I believe that the Conservative approach fails millions of children. It also fails society as a whole too by denying our economy their talents, and by storing up for society a legacy of social, health and community problems too.

Promoting life chances matters

But building social justice involves more than simply a moral crusade against poverty. It is about more than just tackling social exclusion.

103

Plenty of families who feel included in strong communities still don't get a fair deal. Think of the 16 year old in a close family, in a cohesive coalfield community, who doesn't stay on at school because it just isn't what she and her friends ever expected to do. After all staying on rates in coalfield areas are significantly lower than the national average. She isn't excluded from society. She may not have grown up in poverty. And in the short term she may have more cash in her pocket than her peers in leafier suburbs who stay on in education. But she still isn't getting a fair deal. Her chances in life are still dependent on where she lives, and the job her parents do.

So I believe the Fabian Commission in their interim report were right to argue that, 'an exclusive focus on child poverty is too narrow because it leaves out key concerns about broader divisions and inequalities.'

It is the inherited inequalities that cascade from generation to generation that are the most insidious barrier to opportunity. For all that British society seemed to be opening up in the second half of the twentieth century, the miserable truth was that inherited inequalities were as strong as ever by the end of the Conservative years.

So the children born in 1970 actually experienced less social mobility than those born in 1958. Poverty in childhood was more likely to lead to poverty in adulthood for the 1970 generation than for the earlier generation as relative life chances actually fell.

The result is that still at the beginning of the twenty first century, your chances in life depend too much on your parents' income. Children still do not have equal chances in life. Social class still casts a long shadow over British society. Children growing up on low income are still much more likely to end up with lower qualifications, lower wage jobs, suffering unemployment, becoming teenage parents and even dying younger than their classmates from more affluent backgrounds. Children from some ethnic minority groups do persistently worse at school and in the jobs market too, even taking account of family income.

Building a fairer society means we have to address all the barriers to opportunity that people still face. Already Labour in government has made great strides in tackling disadvantage and lack of opportunities, as last year's major Social Exclusion Unit report, Breaking the Cycle, set out.

Staying on rates have gone up, along with rising education standards across the board. The gap between the most deprived districts and the rest in education and employment is starting to narrow. Thousands of lone parents have been helped by the New Deal.

Under the banner of progressive universalism, support has also been extended to widen opportunities and life chances for those on low and average incomes as well as those in poverty. So the Children's Tax Credit provides the greatest support for those on lowest income, but is a considerable boost for average families too. Sure Start has begun in the most deprived areas, but it covers all the children in the area, and the new Children's Centres will reach into every community.

Even though we know that addressing those inherited inequalities will take at least a generation, we are at least starting in the right place—in the early years. We know that the gap in life chances between those growing up in low income families and in more prosperous families is evident even by the age of 22 months. In 1999-2000 I was involved in the Smith Institute work with John Bynner and Heather Joshi looking at life chances among the 1970 and 1958 generation. And their analysis reinforced our decision at that time to pursue a substantial expansion of Sure Start, exactly in order to boost children's life chances. We know however that we will not see the benefits from those extra children helped by Sure Start for many years to come.

Promoting life chances in this way is about more than simply a narrow view of social mobility or equal opportunity. As the Fabian Commission set out in its interim report; 'What concerns us is not merely the fact that talented children from income-poor backgrounds are less likely to realize their potential than those from more affluent families, but that all children from income-poor backgrounds are less likely to realize their potential than those from more affluent families. The goal therefore is to improve the experiences and opportunities for all children and not merely to increase social mobility amongst the most able.'

I think the Fabian Society is right to argue that a modern vision of social justice and equality is a complex one. We have to address the persistence of poverty and the problem of social exclusion. But we also need to widen opportunities for the many families who are not trapped in poverty and who are included in strong local communities, but who just aren't getting a fair deal. We have to tackle inequality of opportunity, and in particular the persistence of inherited inequalities that still cascade from one generation to the next. It isn't enough to simply offer escape routes for a small number of talented children from disadvantaged backgrounds, we have to widen opportunities for every child to fulfil their potential. That has been the Labour approach for the past eight years, now we need to go further.

But again, where are the Conservatives in the debate on raising life chances for all? They have made clear their hostility to expanding numbers in higher education. They have pledged to abolish the New Deal for lone parents – something which is particularly destructive of life chances, because it tackles child poverty and helps mothers back into employment and training at the same time. Given that women on low qualifications were left furthest behind in the social and economic changes of the Conservative years, and given the importance of mothers education and employment to children's development, supporting mothers on low income is one of the most powerful way to improve the life chances of two generations at once. But the Conservatives have opposed it. At best their approach to improving life chances is simply to offer a small number of escape routes for a minority – by using taxpayers money to subsidise their private education. At worst, they are engaged in safeguarding the privileges of the few.

New challenges for the future make this even more important

The challenges we will face over the next few years make the need to promote life chances even more important. The pace of change in the economy and the labour market, the nature of the modern housing market, and the persistent legacy of deep rooted historic attitudes and social relations pose great challenges for our society in the future. And I believe only the Labour party is equipped to address those challenges in the next few years.

Changes in our economy and labour market mean the value of skills and qualifications has increased. But that means the penalty for having no skills or qualifications has increased too, and the risk is that those with poor education can fall further and further behind.

The pace of demand for ever improved qualifications, as well as changes to the structure of the labour market, can make it harder to catch up later on. So research by the Strategy Unit suggests that the changing nature of the modern firm, and the disappearance of many middle management jobs, means it is now harder for people with few qualifications to work their way up through the company from the shop floor. Those who lack a degree when they enter the workforce can find it very hard ever to break into graduate level employment through other routes.

The modern flexible economy means we also need to draw on the talents, potential and entrepreneurship of every individual. But too many people are still held back, both by lack of opportunity and disadvantage, and by deeply embedded attitudes such as lack of confidence among those on low income and persistent prejudice on behalf of others.

The housing market too places new pressures on society. As housing supply has not kept pace with housing demand, house prices have increased. Changing household formation and family break up has contributed too. Low mortgage rates and economic growth have meant we still have over a million more homeowners than in 1997. Nevertheless more people still want to own their own homes. The consequence of a tightening housing market is that while some people inside the housing market have seen their wealth and their assets grow, others outside the housing market are unable to afford the house they want and numbers in temporary accommodation have grown.

Faced with these kinds of challenges, government policy matters

Faced with these kinds of challenges, government policy matters. The wrong kind of policy response could be devastating—not just to the life chances of the most vulnerable, but also to the cohesion of society.

The response of the Conservative government in the eighties and nineties was exactly that. Faced with economic change and restructuring, they did little to support workers losing their jobs, and little to support cities and regions devastated by job losses. Faced with growing returns to education they did little to support widening access to education and skills, in fact the education gap between districts grew. Faced with widening income inequality they did nothing to support families on low income and child poverty trebled.

No one should underestimate the importance of continued economic growth for helping those on lowest skills and lowest income. After all, recessions hit hardest those with least economic power. The impact of the deep recessions of the early eighties and nineties was to knock some workers out of employment not just for a few months but for years at a time. And the social consequences have been considerable too. Children growing up in the eighties on streets where no one worked for years at a time are now parents themselves. Those childhood disadvantages mean they are far more likely to face family problems themselves today. Poverty and troubles in childhood are linked with a wide range of social problems later on, ranging from mental health to drug related crime.

The Conservatives' current policy proposals would be equally damaging, and equally poor at addressing the challenges we face. Cutting investment in key public services won't help. Oliver Letwin has said that outside schools and hospitals, budgets would be frozen. But that would be at the expense of adult education and training—so critical for providing those second and third chances later on in life. More importantly it would prevent the vital expansion of Sure Start children's centres, so important to improving early years.

108

So what should Labour do now?

Labour instead is determined to respond to these new challenges in the labour and housing markets, as well as continuing to tackle the deep rooted historic disadvantages people face. That means equipping families to handle the pressures of a modern economy, and ensuring the economy can make the most of each and everyone's talents and abilities.

In the last four lectures, Alan, David, John and Ruth have already set out key priority areas for a Labour third term. First and foremost it means continuing to tackle the economic root causes of poverty and inequality through helping people into work and cutting child poverty. After all, for all our progress we still have a long way to go.

Secondly it means widening educational opportunities to improve life chances for all—not just in schools, but in those vital early years through Sure Start Children's Centres in every community and later on in life to supporting those crucial second chances people need.

Thirdly it means striving ever harder to break the link between income and wealth on the one hand, and other kinds of life chances such as health. (In contrast to the Conservative approach which strengthens the link by subsidizing private operations.)

Fourthly it means continuing to try to break the link between where you live and your chances in life. Already the New Deal for Communities and Neighbourhood Renewal investment are helping to narrow the gap.

Housing policy

But just as John talked in particular about health and Ruth talked in particular about education, I wanted to say a little more about wealth inequality and the housing market. The strong links between wealth and the housing market, between owning assets and owning your own home, mean that we have to take seriously widening wealth inequality to prevent it becoming a brake on opportunity in the future too.

New analysis by the Social Exclusion Unit shows that for all our progress on other areas, wealth inequality continues to grow. According to Shelter the top 30 per cent of families with children now own 50 per cent of the nation's housing wealth—up from 42 per cent in 1993. In London, over a third of first time buyers rely in part on gifts, family loans, or windfalls. Yet people's chance of owning their own home should not depend on whether their parents and grandparents were homeowners before them.

Already the Child Trust Fund is being increased. The Savings Gateway is being extended. And stamp duty is being abolished on smaller homes. But we need to go further. 70 per cent of the population now own their own homes, with over a million more home owners since 1997, thanks to low mortgage rates and economic stability, in contrast to the boom and bust of the housing market in the eighties and nineties. But 90 per cent say they want to own their homes. With a tightening housing market, many can find themselves denied the chance. Those on lower and middle incomes should not be denied all chance to share in the value of their home, or to get a stake in the property market.

That's why tomorrow, the Chancellor and the Deputy Prime Minister will set out new proposals to help thousands more families buy a share in their home. Labour will help more first time buyers, key workers and social tenants to buy their own home, or even just to buy a share in their home as well. This will extend home ownership opportunities for the first time to thousands who simply cannot afford to get a foothold on the housing ladder right now.

Unlike the Conservatives, we believe we need to do this alongside—and not at the expense of—more homes for those who are most vulnerable. Extending the Right to Buy to Housing Associations, as the Conservatives want to do, would help fewer people in the long run and would cut the availability of social housing and increase homelessness. That is why the new plans to sell shares in social housing are being drawn up with safeguards for social housing, and with receipts invested in new homes to cut homelessness instead.

And it is why we also need to support a big expansion in housing supply as the Sustainable Communities Plan and the Barker Review recommended. Only that way will we be able to respond to the growing demand for housing and the growing pressures on the regional economy too.

Cutting the housing budget by £1 billion as the James Review has proposed, abandoning the Thames Gateway and cutting house building across the South East as the Conservatives have proposed, would have a very detrimental effect on life chances for families across London and the South East. It would restrict the affordability of housing to many families, and would push up numbers in temporary accommodation too.

It would also badly restrain the regional economy, and therefore the prosperity of many more families besides. Restricting house building as the Conservatives wish to do serves only to protect the interests of those home owners who will see their house prices continue to rise, and who are wealthy enough to be insulated from the wider pressures affecting the regional economy too.

Promoting home ownership is often seen as being about aspirations. It is. But it is also about addressing inequalities. And when done alongside expanding housing supply and improving access to social housing too, it forms a vital part of a programme to widen life chances for all.

And we need to build that progressive consensus

Finally, as the Fabian Commission has made clear, and as David set out in the first lecture of this series, we need to entrench the battle against poverty and unjust inequalities in a new political settlement.

After eight years in government I believe Labour has already changed the debate about poverty and social exclusion in Britain. Ten years ago, Conservative politicians now regarded as relatively moderate were still able to attack and vilify those who were most disadvantaged. Remember Peter Lilley on the subject of single parents or Sir George Young on the subject of rough sleepers? Now even the most right wing Conservative politicians and commentators dare not publicly propose slashing Children's Tax Credits, Sure Start or action to address social exclusion.

It is a sign of how far the Conservative party think the consensus in the country has changed that Michael Howard has been so neurotic in response to Howard Flight's statement of what is widely believed to be the reality behind their plans. Yet even the Conservatives recognize that the public have no appetite for a return to Thatcherism.

Of course the Fabian Society is right that there is still limited awareness among the wider public about the progress made and the challenges remaining in cutting child poverty. But when faced with the evidence, people do support action to cut poverty and improve children's chances in life. We have not yet gone far enough. Just as we have more to do to address poverty and unjust inequality in Britain, we have more to do to build a progressive consensus of support around our programme too.

It shouldn't just be in the months before an election that Tories fear to mention cutting public spending. It shouldn't just be when seeking votes that they fear to criticize support for families.

The 1945 Labour government built an NHS that the Conservatives have feared to challenge for decades. So the next Labour government needs to extend the welfare state to the under 5s, so that the very ethos of our welfare state and our public institutions is to tackle disadvantage in the very young and to give every child the very best start in life.

The NHS has served to nurture and sustain the values of fairness and equity which underpinned its very establishment in the first place — that health care should be provided according to need and not ability to pay. Similarly we need our Children's Centres to embody and embed important values of fairness — promoting the life chances of every child. Politicians of the right should fear to cut the children's centres of the future, just as today they fear to admit to cuts in the NHS because they know the strength of public feeling.

And we need to build a consensus across the country in support of cutting child poverty and widening life chances for all. We still need to do more to persuade people that the inequalities we face undermine social justice for all of us. Giving every child a fair chance in life is an imperative for every modern civilized society.

112

I believe this is a cause which should command broad support across society. After all it is about improving opportunities for the many, not preserving the privileges of the few. It taps into people's aspirations for themselves and their families, their desire to learn, to create and to get on. But it also reflects people's sense of responsibility to their community and to others, and the moral sense that everyone should be treated with equal respect, and no one should be unfairly excluded from the opportunities and life chances that others take for granted. Furthermore it helps us to address the economic challenges we face, by promoting the talents and creativity of all our citizens. And it helps reduce the difficult social consequences of a divided and distressed society too.

In the last eight years, the Labour government has made great strides in tackling many of the worst aspects of poverty and inequality in modern Britain. But we still have much to do. Our challenge now is to forge a third term programme, and a political cause for the nation based on sustaining that progress. This is our chance to build a society in which individuals receive equal respect and children gain from equal opportunities and life chances and in which the cycle of disadvantage from generation to generation is truly broken.

Response by Sukhvinder Stubbs

My growing cynicism about the ability of this or any government in establishing a progressive agenda has been to some extent tempered by the eloquent and passionate comments made by Yvette Cooper. When she speaks of the need to entrench the battle against poverty and unjust inequalities in a new political settlement, there is a sense that she actually means it. These days, it is rare to hear politicians talk about moral causes. When the Barrow Cadbury Trust agreed to support this Commission, the discussion about 'life chances' was not commonplace. So, just a few months on, it is heartening to see it feature so prominently in the contemplations of such influential ministers. The recognition that inequality and disadvantage are passed down generations and that life chances in early years are critical in breaking the cycle is long overdue but most welcome. While

113

Yvette should be justly proud of the achievements of the government, she is also right to say that more needs to be done.

The target to abolish child poverty by 2020 is one of the most radical actions taken by this government. Actually achieving this remains one of their biggest challenges. Research indicates that any government wishing to stay on target for eradicating child poverty by 2020 will need to spend at least an extra £2 billion per year by 2007/8. At a time when Labour are under pressure to reduce public spending, it requires an unprecedented level of confidence and commitment for the government to go to the public and ask for more. Understandably, this is currently lacking. They fear a public backlash with accusations of waste, of over-spending, of special treatment conferred to special needs groups determined by an agenda of political correctness. But the truth is that the public displays far more empathy for the poor than the government would credit them. At a work-shop organised to assess how public attitudes to poverty could be influenced, it became clear from the outset that most people aren't even aware of the govern-ment's stated intention to end child poverty. All of the participants, including those who had been sceptical at the outset, thought that a monthly £20 raise of income tax would be acceptable (this would be the equivalent of a 2 per cent increase for someone on an average salary). A handful of participants even agreed on £50 extra a month. Although poverty is not the sort of issue that is going to make headline news, it is clear that most people do have a strong sense of social justice and fairness, which does not take much to induce.

It was however disappointing that the Minister did not say more about the life chances of ethnic minorities. When it comes to government policy, there continues to be a glaring absence of any analysis on race and poverty. The life chances framework provides an opportunity for tackling racial injustice. As impor-tant as the equal opportunities agenda is, it kicks in much later in life; essentially it is for adults. It aims to provide redress in unfair treatment but can do little to ensure those opportunities are equally available to all from the outset. Life chances should ensure that whether a child is born black or white, rich or poor, they have the same spread of opportunities ahead of them. A level playing field is best secured at birth, not in adulthood. A clear policy on race and poverty is missing and this is certainly one of the areas that Barrow Cadbury is researching.

Much has been made of Labour's emphasis on asset ownership. After all, which of us home owning middle class would argue against the merits of this? But is there an element of inconsistency in the plans to extend home ownership? Yvette's assertion that social housing had to be protected and enhanced goes without saying. Of course we need to ensure that the supply of social housing is extended so that homelessness is not forced up. However, there is also a concern that expanses of social housing helped to create ghettos of poverty. If Yvette is serious about no one being disadvantaged by where they live, then communities of poor people need to be folded among those of relative advantage. Few people know this but the early 70s saw the arrival of a group of Kenyans in the Birmingham district of Handsworth, where I grew up. They were much more skilled than their poor, largely rural Pakistani, Caribbean and Sikh neighbours. More importantly, they aspired to greater things. Their entrepreneurialism not only benefited the Kenyans, who soon moved on, but also helped the opportunistic Sikh communities who were able to latch on to the coat tails of the Kenyan professionals and entrepreneurs.

Sadly these days, current punitive policies on migration mean that there is little chance of interventions of this sort in the future. However, desegregation has to be a viable option. As honourable as it is for Yvette to support the Housing Association movement in protecting supply, geographic concentration is not the best way forward. What is needed is for the expansion of affordable housing to include replacement social housing but not en bloc. Research indicates that communities can absorb 10-20 per cent social housing—beyond that, the environment becomes unsustainable.

Yvette Cooper sets out a laudable and plausible argument for a government committed to improving life chances. But when she says that the government need to go further, it's not public attitudes that are the inhibiting factor but courage, conviction and commitment on the government's part—in essence the critical elements of leadership.

Sukhvinder Stubbs is Director of the Barrow Cadbury Trust

References

i   BSAS also asked respondents whether they thought taxes for those on high, middle and low incomes were too high or low, then asked which of these groups respondents thought they were in. In 1995 only 4 per cent of those who said they were middle income and 3 per cent who said they were low income felt that their own taxes were too low. Fewer than 3 per cent of the sample described themselves as having a high income. Almost nobody thought that their personal tax levels were too low. In short, therefore, there was general agreement that it was other people's taxes that should go up.

ii   For the Fabian Commission on Life Chances and Child Poverty, MORI conducted two group discussions, a three hour extended focus group and a full day workshop on 2nd and 6th February 2005 respectively. The focus group comprised 9 people and lasted 3 hours whilst the workshop comprised 21 participants and lasted 6 hours. In both discussions, a representative sample was recruited on the basis of gender, BME status, and age/lifestage within the range 25-45 years (focus group) and 25-65 years (workshop). All participants were drawn from socio-economic classes BC1C2, and participants' professional sectors included teaching, insurance, social work, banking, and leisure. Participants were also screened on the basis of party political affiliation, newspaper readership and the level of priority they attached to the issue of child poverty in Britain. The objective here was to exclude people who were identifiable as strongly on the left or right of the political spectrum. For practical reasons, however, all were recruited from London and the South East of England. They should not be taken as a representative sample of UK citizens, therefore; but the results of the deliberative research can nonetheless give us useful pointers towards directions for the debate on child poverty and life chances which may chime more or less well with the concerns of people 'in the middle' of the political landscape.

References

iii   The Eurobarometer surveys have asked questions about perceived
        causes of poverty since 1976, distinguishing between personal
        causes of poverty ('because they've been unlucky' and 'because of
        laziness or lack of willpower') and social causes ('because there's a
        great deal of injustice in our society' and 'it's inevitable in the
        modern world').

iv   DWP (2004). Opportunity for All: Sixth Annual Report, 2004. TSO.
        http://www.dwp.gov.uk/ofa/reports/2004/pdf/report_04.pdf

v   Vegeris, S & Perry, J. (2003). Families and children 2001: Living
        standards and the children. DWP Research Report No.—190. Leeds:
        CDS. http://www.psi.org.uk/docs/2003/news-FACS-DWP-sum-
        190.pdf

vi   UNICEF (2005) Child Poverty in Rich Countries 2005, Innocenti
        Report Card no.6 press release.

vii   Marsh, A. (2001) Ending Child Poverty: Inaugural Lecture delivered at
        the University of Westminster on 10 March 2004. Available at:
        http://www.psi.org.uk/docs/2004/alanmarsh.pdf.

viii   Kempson, E. (1996). Life on a Low Income. Joseph Rowntree
        Foundation. Quote from p.49. This review brings together the find-
        ings of more than 30 qualitative studies on what life is like for a
        range of people on low incomes including two-parent families and
        lone mothers in low paid work and/or on means tested benefit.

ix   Gregg, P., Waldfogel, J. & Washbrook, E. (2005). 'That's the way
        the Money Goes: Expenditure Patterns as Real Income Rise for the
        Poorest Families with Children' in Hills, J. & Stewart, K. (eds) An
        Equal Society? New Labour, Poverty, Inequality and Exclusion. Policy
        Press.

x   Middleton, S., Ashworth, K. & Braithwaite, I. (1997). Small Fortunes:
        Spending on Children, Childhood Poverty and Parental Sacrifice. York:
        Joseph Rowntree Foundation.

xi   Middleton, S., Ashworth, K. & Walker, R. (1994). Family Fortunes:
        Pressures on Parents & Children in the 1990s. London: CPAG.

xii   Kempson, E. (1996). P.37.

118

xiii   Utting, D. (1995) Family and Parenthood: Supporting families, preventing breakdown—A guide to the debate. York: Joseph Rowntree Foundation.

xiv   Childhood Poverty and Material Deprivation: Findings from the 1999 Poverty and Social Exclusion Survey. Bradshaw, J., Middleton, S., Williams, J. and Ashworth, K. (2000) The Necessities of Life for Children, Working Paper 2, Available at: http://www.bris.ac.uk/poverty/pse.

xv   ONS (2002). Trends in life expectancy by social class 1972–1999. ONS. http://www.statistics.gov.uk/downloads/theme_population/ Life_Expect_Social_class_1972-99/Life_Expect_Social_class_1972-99.pdf

xvi   ONS (2004). Social Trends, Number 34, London. TSO. http://www.statistics.gov.uk/downloads/theme_social/Social_Trends34/Social_Trends34.pdf

xvii   ONS (2004). The Health of Children and Young People. TSO. http://www.statistics.gov.uk/children/

xviii   ONS (2004). See reference viii.

xix   DfES (2004). Trends in Education & Skills, DfES website. http://www.dfes.gov.uk/trends/index.cfm

xx   Shelter (2004). Know Your Place: Housing Wealth and Inequality in Great Britain 1980-2003 and Beyond. http://england.shelter.org.uk/files/docs/7970/Knowyourplace.pdf

xxi   Longitudinal research is valuable for highlighting changes and continuities in outcomes from childhood to adulthood for different groups of children. However, the major limitations are that it cannot provide conclusive evidence on causation, due to the complex web of factors and processes (some of which may not have been included in the original surveys). Also, different factors may become more or less important at different stages of the life course. SEU (2004). The Impact of Government Policy on Social Exclusion Among Young People. ODPM. http://www.socialexclusion.gov.uk/downloaddoc.asp? id=268

119

References

xxii   Hobcraft, J. (2003). Continuity and Change in Pathways to Young Adult Disadvantage: Results from a British Birth Cohort. CASE Paper 66. Centre for Analysis of Social Exclusion, London School of Economics. http://sticerd.lse.ac.uk/dps/case/cp/CASEpaper66.pdf

xxiii   Ermicsh, J., Francesconi, M., and Pevalin, D.J. (2001). Outcomes for Children of Poverty, DWP Research Report 158. Leeds: CDS. http://www.dwp.gov.uk/asd/asd5/rport158/Main.pdf

xxiv   Feinstein, L. (2003). 'Inequality in the Early Cognitive Development of British Children in the 1970 Cohort,' Economica, 70: 73-97.

xxv   Marsh, A. (2004) Ending child poverty: Inaugural lecture by Alan Marsh, delivered at the University of Westminster, 10 March 2004. Available at: http://www.psi.org.uk/docs/2004/alanmarsh.pdf

xxvii   (Rutter, M. (1974), 'Dimensions of parenthood: some myths and some suggestions', in The Family in Society: Dimensions of Parenthood, Dept of Health and Social Security, HMSO.)

Terms of Reference

The Commission aims to make a major contribution to the future development of the government's strategy to end child poverty and to reframe the public debate on this issue. Using a 'life chances' framework, the research will consider both practical policy solutions to child poverty, and the more theoretical underpinnings of the strategy. The focus will be on some or all of the following: income and occupation, health and well-being, education, environmental quality, security and safety, aspirations, and the ability to make decisions about one's own life in relation to social position. An important part of the project will be to explore the experiences and views of families with experience of poverty themselves.

The Commission will address specifically:

■ Ways of conceptualising child poverty within a life chances framework: **what do poverty, equality and mobility mean in contemporary Britain?**

■ The character and performance of existing anti-poverty interventions: **is the government's strategy appropriate for the challenge?**

■ The experience of other countries in addressing child poverty: **are there lessons to be learned from taking an international perspective?**

■ Ways in which the stated aim of ending child poverty can best be achieved: **what more needs to be done to meet the Prime Minister's ambitious target?**

The Commission's final report—including policy recommendations—will be published in Autumn 2005.